Frank Harrison and Joan Rimmer

European musical instruments

W. W. Norton & Company, Inc. · New York

Contents

Preface

The aim of this book is to provide a brief chronological account of the musical instruments of Western man from the earliest records of their use to the present day.

The story of musical instruments is inseparable from that of instrumental music. The history of Western music has usually been written largely in terms of recorded notation. The history of instruments, however, is recorded in the fabric of the instruments – in why and how they were made, how and where they were played – as well as in the symbols of the music they sounded. For much of the history of European music there are no symbols, and instruments, their iconography and their folk survivals, are almost the only evidence we possess.

In the text we have tried to co-ordinate the history of instruments with the history of music, while the illustrations provide visual evidence of their forms and uses. In a book of this scope complete coverage of all instruments is not possible. For fuller details about some art instruments, and about variants of folk instruments and their distribution, the reader is referred to specialized publications cited in the footnotes.

We are grateful to all the institutions, makers and private owners who appear in the list of Acknowledgments for their courtesy and co-operation in making photographs available. We also wish to thank Mr Anthony Baines of Uppingham School, Mr O. W. Neighbour of the British Museum and Mr P. F. Ganz of Hertford College, Oxford, for information and help, and Mr J. V. S. Megaw of the University of Sydney for expert advice on European prehistory.

Oxford, 1964   F. H. & J. R.

1 Prehistory

How can we tell anything at all about the music made by prehistoric man? In the absence of written symbols his music and his speech, unlike his painting and his artifacts, have no record. However, among his artifacts are some he used for making musical sounds. These scattered remains are the only direct evidence we possess about the music of European prehistory. While comparison of prehistoric instruments with those of relevant cultures, both past and present, may suggest many analogies, it is not a safe basis for firm deductions about the music of prehistory. Musical responses vary with climate and physical surroundings, with the requirements for survival, and with the kinds of raw material which lie to hand. Contact with contemporary peoples, whether more or less advanced, is bound to bring new ideas and to affect the course of development. Even if we assume some normal pattern of historical change, it was not always from the simple to the complex; at times it was the reverse.

It is not even a safe assumption that all peoples use instruments to make sound. The Vedda of Ceylon and some Patagonian tribes have no musical instruments, nor do they even clap their hands or stamp the ground[1]. Not all ethnic groups use all the basic types of instrument. The Australian aborigines and the Fuegians do not make flutes – Anthony Baines has called them the 'flute-less advance-guards of mankind'[2]. It is certain, however, that prehistoric man in Europe made 'flutes', and it is intriguing that the earliest surviving examples come from the same time and from the same places as the earliest works of visual art we possess [1]. These earliest survivals are one-note 'flutes', perhaps actually decoy-whistles, made of the toe-bones of reindeer; they were found in the painted caves of Spain and south-western France and in other Upper Palaeolithic sites [2]. These distant ancestors of the ocarina were blown across the hole from the end of the bone above the cleavage, and they have been called 'globular' flutes. When the player blows across a hole, in this prehistoric instrument as in the modern transverse flute, he directs his breath against the further edge of the hole; this demands considerable skill. In another kind of flute which also survives from prehistory – the fipple flute [3, 4], ancestor of the recorder – the skill required in playing is small, but the making of the instrument requires both acoustical awareness and competent craftsmanship. The insertion into the upper end of the tube of a plug (fipple) slightly smaller than the aperture creates a narrow wind-channel, through which the player's breath is automatically directed against the further edge of a small 'window' cut into the tube just below the plug. Palaeolithic man almost certainly knew not only these two ways of

[1] The superior figures refer to the notes at the end of each chapter; figures in square brackets refer to illustrations.

making sound, but also the two basic ways of making a series of different notes with one instrument. Finger-holes, which alter the operative length of the tube and therefore give a series of different notes from one tube, must have been a revolutionary discovery. The other way, more obvious though not necessarily earlier in time, was to use a separate tube for each note, making what Greek mythology later named panpipes [20].

From Neolithic times we have fipple flutes made of the bones of birds or animals, with holes pierced in one or both sides, that is, with finger-holes and thumb-hole[3]. Found in various parts of eastern and western Europe, these finger-hole flutes show that Stone Age man, like many primitive peoples today, had a pragmatic acquaintance with the acoustical behaviour of hollow objects, and a technology in fashioning his materials which presupposes uncharted ages of development before his time. The most frequent number of finger-holes in prehistoric fipple flutes is three, perhaps because it is a convenient number to manage with one hand. The discovery of a Neolithic three-hole fipple flute of hollowed stag's antler in a gallery grave near Poitiers was recorded in 1869 by François Fétis, head of the Brussels Conservatoire and one of the pioneers of musicology[4]; another Neolithic flute, found in a cave in Istria, was made from a human thigh-bone. Sets of pipes of unequal length which were certainly sounded in the manner of panpipes have also been found[5].

European man continued to make flutes of bone and similar material through the Bronze and Iron Ages and in medieval and modern times. Bronze Age examples include one found at Normanton Down in Wiltshire and now in the Devizes Museum, and a three-hole flute, the earliest in Britain, found in a grave from a burial mound near Avebury, which is a lesser Stonehenge. An Iron Age specimen, found at Malham Tarn in the West Riding of Yorkshire and now in the Leeds Museum, was made from the right tibia of a sheep; it has two holes in front and one at the back[6]. From Roman times at least nine bone flutes have been excavated in the city of London[7] and several elsewhere in northern Europe. A bone fipple flute of the second half of the thirteenth century found at White Castle, Monmouthshire[8], and a four-hole pipe found under the floor of a farm built in 1869 at Paarup in Denmark[9], illustrate the continuity of this simple type in northern Europe.

The basic change in mode of life between the Palaeolithic and the Neolithic Ages has been described as a change from 'hunting to husbandry'[10]. Man began to settle in permanent village communities, and this brought new crafts, new discoveries and the use of new materials. Although the archaeological evidence so far cannot be conclusive, it is very likely that the vertical open-ended flute was one of these discoveries; its earliest representation is on a slate of the fourth millennium B.C. from Hierakonpolis in Egypt[11]. To sound this kind of flute the player blows across the top of the vertically held open pipe [5, 6] – the most difficult of all blowing techniques. In the hands of virtuosi such as are still found in Turkey and the Balkans it produces a more brilliant and expressive sound than is possible on any fipple flute. (The question of these relative capacities of fipple and non-fipple flutes became specially important in the eighteenth century in connection with the recorder and the transverse flute.)

A different way of producing sound is used in what may be called 'loose-lip' instruments, which include the brass of today. Here the player presses his lips against a relatively large aperture tightly enough to exclude air, and his lips themselves vibrate under the pressure of his breath. It is probably safe to assume that prehistoric man sounded large hollow objects in this fashion. With a conch-shell the small end serves as the mouthpiece while the spiral forms the tube [7]. Its sound is powerful and far-carrying, and in Greek mythology a Triton was said to conquer giants with the terrifying sound of a conch-shell trumpet. It is still used as a means of announcing their wares by fish-sellers in Majorca, and as a fiesta sound-maker by the citizens of Naples.

With the Neolithic stage and the making of domestic pottery, the acoustic behaviour of hollow pots must have been noticed. Many Neolithic pottery drums have been discovered in central Europe[12], and reconstructions of one pair [8] have produced a sound comparable with that of pottery drums which still survive in the Balkans and elsewhere. Pottery rattles, presumably derived from vegetable prototypes, have been found in children's graves of the late Neolithic period in Czechoslovakia. Judging by their shape, they were predecessors of the rattles of the Bronze Age [13]. Palaeolithic man had used the natural material of bone to make sounds by friction; a bone scraper has been found in the same Palaeolithic cave in Moravia as specimens of globular flute and fipple flute[13]. According to Sachs the rather mysterious half-scraper half-drum known as the friction drum belongs to the late Neolithic period[14]. In its normal form a friction drum is a hollow vessel covered by a membrane, with a central hole in which a stick or thread is rubbed up and down. In primitive societies it is associated with fertility rites, and it may possibly have been so used by Neolithic man in Europe. In modern Europe it survives only as a noise-maker in fiesta and fairground [9, 10].

Marius Schneider has said that 'primitive man sings only when he has something definite to express', and that 'even his instrumental melody and his whistling are the expression of definite ideas'[15]. From flutes with finger-holes we can get a rough idea of the scales which prehistoric man used for his tunes. The two which have been most thoroughly studied from this point of view are an Upper Palaeolithic fipple flute made from the femur of a cave bear from the Hungarian cave site of Istallosko, and the Iron Age example from Malham Tarn. Both have two holes on the front side and one on the back. The scale given by the Malham pipe is the Dorian tetrachord of Greek music[16]. However, it is a long way from a scale to a tune; there is no way of telling whether primitive man modified the notes of his flutes by partial closing of the holes, by over-blowing, or by varying his lip tension. But something of what he is likely to have expressed may be deduced from the contexts in which musical instruments have been found. The Upper Palaeolithic specimens come from the rock shelter dwellings of hunting men, where paintings were produced almost certainly as part of a magic ritual to ensure a successful hunt[17]; the disguised figure in plate I seems to be using the instrument, if that is what it is, to gain power over the animals he hunts. In a later pastoral society the music of a flute would have whiled away the hours for a shepherd or called his flock together, as it still does for an Aegean or Pyrenean shepherd. With the development of urban communities and the discovery of new methods of making musical sounds, fipple flutes and panpipes became associated with rustic and pastoral people, and have remained so ever since.

1 C.Sachs, *The History of Musical Instruments*, 1940, p. 26.

2 *Woodwind Instruments and their History*, 1962, p. 171.

3 J.V.S.Megaw, 'Penny Whistles and Prehistory', *Antiquity*, xxxiv, 1960, pp. 6–13.

4 *Histoire générale de la Musique*, i, 1869, pp. 25–6, figs. 3–4, cited by Megaw, p. 9.

5 J.V.S.Megaw, 'Penny Whistles and Prehistory: Further Notes', *Antiquity*, xxxv, 1961, p. 56.

6 A.Raistrick, Prof. Spaul, E.Todd, 'The Malham Iron-Age Pipe', *Galpin Society Journal*, v, 1952, p. 28.

7 Sir Mortimer Wheeler, 'London in Roman Times', *London Museum Catalogues*, 3, 1946, p. 107, pl. xlvii B, cited by Megaw, p. 11.

8 Megaw, 'A Medieval Bone Pipe from White Castle, Monmouthshire', *Galpin Society Journal*, xvi, 1963, p. 85.

9 Megaw in *Antiquity*, xxxiv, 1960, p. 11.

10 H.W.Janson, *A History of Art*, 1962, p. 22.

11 Sachs, op. cit., p. 90.

12 A.Buchner, *Musical Instruments through the Ages*, 1956, pl. 6–7.

13 Ibid., pl. 1–5.

14 Op. cit., p. 64.

15 E.Wellesz, ed., *The New Oxford History of Music*, i, 1957, p. 2.

16 Megaw, pp. 11–12.

17 Janson, op. cit., p. 19.

2 *Ancient civilizations and their decline*

While central and northern Europe were still in the Neolithic stage, great city civilizations had already grown up in the Near East, with complex and hierarchical social structures and advanced technology in precious metals. Though archaeology is beginning to discover the extent of these vanished high civilizations, we have no knowledge of the stages of discovery and development between the simple musical instruments of Neolithic man and the already sophisticated instruments of the Sumerians, and Babylonians. These peoples made music with the sounds of vibrating strings and reeds; fipple flutes and panpipes must already have been rustic instruments. Even apart from the splendour of their gold and silver casings, the lyres of Ur of about 2,500 B.C. are elaborately assembled artifacts[1]; they consist of a resonance chamber or soundbox, two arms which support the string-carrying yoke, and eight to eleven strings fixed over a bridge. While the double pipes of the ancient Near East, now generally known by their Greek name of *aulos*, were not complicated in structure, the fashioning and controlling of the reeds, whether single or double, by which they were sounded, were mature musical techniques far removed from any known Neolithic practice. Less sophisticated as instruments, though advanced in metal technology, are the silver trumpets such as those found in the tomb of Tut-ankh-amon (*c* 1350 B.C.), and the sistrum, a metal form of the primitive frame rattle. The latter was used in Minoan Crete [12], though seemingly in quite a different context from its high-cult use in Egyptian religion. It is still used in one of the oldest Christian liturgies, that of the Coptic Church of Egypt and Ethiopia, countries in which lyres of ancient type also survive.

There was a considerable gap in time before the refined technology of the ancient Near East was matched in northern Europe. With the growth of the Aegean civilizations amber was brought from Jutland, and tin from Cornwall and Bohemia; by the same routes in reverse metalware and the knowledge of metalwork were distributed in Italy and central Europe, in the west Baltic and the British Isles[2]. Of the known musical products of the northern European Bronze Age the most important were the 'horns' (called *lurs* in Denmark) of which many examples have survived[3]. The forms of horn and trumpet derive respectively from the horn of an animal and the tube of a cane or hollow branch. Hence the horn is a tube of generally conical shape, the trumpet of cylindrical shape, often with a funnel or flared bell-shaped end. Bronze 'horns' were made in one or more pieces in a simple horn shape, or in a coiled horn shape with flat decorated discs added at the end; coiled horns were probably used ritually in pairs; and there is evidence for the use of pairs of lurs at human sacrifices. In the *carnyx*, which was the war trumpet of the Iron Age Celts, the bell was fashioned into the shape of a horrific animal's head[4].

We have some knowledge of the mouthpieces of the Bronze Age instruments (some are side-blown and do not require them), but none of the music played on them. However, instruments of markedly different sizes and proportions must have been used for different functions. That some of the instruments were capable of sounding a number of notes of the harmonic series is no indication that their full capabilities were used. If the craft of blowing measured up to the craftsmanship of making, they probably were, but this cannot be assumed.

The relation of the musical customs and instruments of the northern Europeans with those of the Near East and Mediterranean is still an under-explored subject. Climatic conditions and the resulting differences in modes of living certainly have a bearing on this. It is suggestive, for example, that northern wind instruments seem to derive from animal-horn shapes, those of the south from prototypes in vegetable material. With the Greeks we come to a later civilization based on life in cities, one which grew by conquest and colonization until it spread from Sicily and southern Italy to the west coast of Caucasia. The population of ancient Greece was made up of a number of originally separate tribes – the main groups were the Dorians, Ionians and Phrygians. Besides such indigenous music as these component groups may have had, the Greeks assimilated most of the musical practices and instruments of the other great civilizations of the Near East. From Homer's *Iliad* we know that the lyre, kithara and aulos were current instruments by the ninth century B.C.[5] From the seventh century B.C., when Greek urban civilization was fully established, vase painting has provided a lavish iconographical documentation of instruments and their place in Greek life.

The Greek lyre [15] (with its allied form the kithara [16]) was a smaller and less splendid instrument than the lyre of the more ancient Near East. Its soundbox was often made of tortoiseshell covered with skin, its arms of naturally curved animal horn or of wood. The strings were fixed to the yoke over rolls of leather which were twisted to alter the tension – a rather cumbersome method of tuning. Kithara strings were sometimes fixed to the yoke over small rods, which could be levered up and down. (Both forms of string fixing survive in certain African lyres.) The strings – three or four in Homeric times, increased to nine to twelve by the fifth century – were tuned it is thought[6] in a pentatonic scale (five notes to the octave). While the lyre was used for teaching and for accompanying lyric poetry, the kithara was the solo instrument of professionals and the accompanying instrument for the chanting of epic poetry.

Aulos means pipe. Historically the term probably covered reed instruments (not flutes, as it has been persistently mistranslated) from the primitive cane tube incorporating its own single reed [17] to the Greek and Roman instrument with two pipes and detachable double reeds [18]. The two pipes of the aulos were generally played at an angle to each other. From the Elgin pair [19], the most complete surviving specimens of the time of Plato, it has been deduced that each pipe was tuned in a pentatonic scale like the stringed instruments, and that the player was able to cover the range of an octave on each pipe. We have little knowledge of later aulos tunings; surviving examples are fragmentary or fragile, and there has been a lack of the necessary knowledge of reed-making among past researchers in this field.

Though small in compass, the Greek aulos had the low pitch in relation to its length which is characteristic of all cylindrical reed instruments[7]. It was undoubtedly an instrument with an exciting and richly sonorous sound. Some idea of the range of the musical capabilities of pipes of this kind may be grasped from performances on the Caucasian *duduk* [26], a folk survival in which the two pipes are played by separate players. The effects produced by Georgian and Armenian players on this instrument are very different, the former's music being virile and exciting, the latter's melancholy and introverted. The ancient Greek aulos-player's technique of non-stop playing, which involved simultaneous breathing in through the nose and blowing, placed great strain on the cheek muscles – hence the cheek-straps seen in so many depictions. Another method of ensuring continuous sound is to attach a reservoir of air which can be forced through the pipe – as in the bagpipe. This instrument is not clearly documented until late Roman times, but may well have existed earlier.

As to the physical possibilities of the double aulos, the player could do any one of three things: play the same tune on both pipes so that they reinforced each other; play a melody on one and a drone on the other; play two-part music. There is no real reason to doubt that he did in fact do the last two of these, if one may judge from the folk use of double and triple pipes today. Anthony Baines has written in this connection: '. . . it is across the old Greek area, from the Black Sea to Italy and Sardinia, that living double-pipe tradition today exhibits an intricate mixture of drone and polyphony that is approached nowhere else in the world of folk music'[8]. It is commonly held that Greek music did not use 'true polyphony', but to say this is almost certainly to narrow the sense of the general term polyphony to mean western European counterpoint. The player of the Sardinian triple *launeddas*, for example, plays in two parts plus drone[9], as does the player of the Sicilian *zampogna*, a bagpipe with two divergent melody pipes (chanters) and two drones[10].

The relation between the cults and religious observances of ancient Greece and the practice of instrumental music is a neglected subject. It seems likely that the use of instruments of the drum and tambour type was virtually confined to certain cults, while concussion instruments such as *krotala* [14] and small cymbals [24, 25] were used more generally for the self-accompaniment of dancers.

The alleged degeneration of music in education and in society which Plato, writing in the mid-fourth century B.C., lamented so bitterly, reflected increasing complication in composition and performance, the rise of professional virtuosi, and the relegation of the mass of music-lovers to the status of listeners. It was in this situation, a recurring one in certain phases of any society, that Plato formulated his doctrine of *ethos*, the effect of music on the soul. Although it gave occasion for some nonsense, as when an attack of sciatica was said to be cured by playing on the aulos a tune in the Phrygian mode above the affected part[11], it had a basic sense which we still instinctively recognize when we refrain from playing Mendelssohn's Wedding March at a funeral.

On the Italian mainland the civilization of Etruria, like that of the Greeks, was based on cities, and prospered on the basis of a commercial empire which rivalled the Greeks' in the western Mediterranean. Etruscan art depicts instruments which were also used by the Greeks [20] but with more emphasis on instruments made of metal [21], which was one of the sources of Etruscan wealth. The music of the Romans began under the triple influence of Greece, Etruria and the Near East. In 204 B.C. the cult of Cybele, the Great Mother, was brought to Rome from Phrygia during the dark days of the second Punic war[12], and the eunuch priests brought with them the Phrygian aulos and other instruments for the ritual of the goddess [22]. The Phrygian aulos associated with the cult had divergent pipes of unequal length and an upturned bell on the longer pipe – a feature found in many folk pipes and in the medieval hornpipe and in the pibcorn [77, 78]. Several aulos (Latin *tibia*) forms, made in wood or bone, jointed or in one piece, and in later times sometimes covered with bronze, were ultimately co-existent [24, 27, 28].

In the late Republic and under the emperors, Roman urban life was organized on a scale unknown to the Greeks. The relation between Rome and classical Greece was roughly comparable to that between the New World and the Old in this century. The huge Roman armies needed signalling instruments for camp and battle organization. Three of these instruments had Etruscan prototypes – the straight *tuba* and looped *cornu* [23], used in battle, and the hooked *lituus* [21], used also on ceremonial occasions. The small and rarely depicted *bucina* was the 'bugle' of the Roman army, for sounding watches and other administrative signals. (In contrast to these, the Greeks' only 'brass' instrument was the short *salpinx*.) The Roman 'brass' instruments were also played in the amphitheatre with the powerful organ, *hydraulis* [23]. Invented in the third century B.C. in Alexandria, then a centre of science and engineering, the hydraulis used a metal bell in water to change the intermittent air pressure from a piston pump into the even air pressure required to blow pipes. The player's 'keyboard' actuated slides which admitted air to the pipes[13]. A spectacle of modern tattoo proportions in A.D. 284 had a hundred tuba-players, a hundred players of the cornu and a hundred tibia-players[14]. The tibia was played at concerts, on convivial occasions and at ritual sacrifices. Whereas in the classical Greek theatre the aulos had the practical function of leading in the chorus, the realism of the farcical mimes and danced pantomimes of the Roman theatre was backed by a variety of sounds, including panpipes, stringed instruments, cymbals and drums, as well as tibiae.

The attitude of the early Christians to musical instruments was so strongly anti-pagan that all instruments were excluded from the ritual, and most from the language of religious symbolism. Accepted in symbolism, though not in ritual, were the panpipes of David as shepherd [29], the plucked-string instruments, real or fanciful, of David as king and psalmist [32, 33, 37–9, 41, 44, 46, 47], and the trump of doom. The percussion and reed instruments which had been so closely associated with pagan cults were completely banned. The world of reed instruments was changed not only by reason of Christian disapproval, but by the fundamental discovery that a conical pipe sounded by a reed gives by overblowing a second series of notes an octave higher than the first. This produces an instrument of much greater continuous range than any cylindrical pipe, which when overblown (we have no certain evidence that the pipes of antiquity were) gives a series of notes an octave-plus-a-fifth higher than the first, leaving a gap between the two series (see below, pp. 36–7). According to Sachs a conical reed instrument was depicted as early as A.D. 132–5 on Jewish coins issued during a revolt against the Emperor Hadrian[15]. Centuries later it was one of the chief Arab instruments, and its use spread with Arab influence into medieval Europe, where it was called in English shalmye, later shawm and hoboy.

Fingerboard instruments (lute is the generic term, as well as the particular name for one of the group), in which strings are stopped by the fingers to give notes of different pitch, were common in ancient Egypt. They were rare in western Europe even in late Roman times [28]. Like conical reed instruments, lutes were important in the music of Arab high civilization and they probably reached western Europe first through contact in Moorish Spain [33].

The sensuous instrumental music of Greek and Roman religion and drama sank almost without trace with the fall of Rome, the barbarian conquests and Christian disapproval. The early Church was preoccupied with liturgical practice, with the nature of chant, and with monasticism; it had no ritual instrumental music comparable with that of Greek and Roman religion. The organ, however, respectably ancient but not specifically associated with pagan ritual, was acceptable to Christians. Loud and imposing in sound, and mechanically fairly complex, it also had great rarity value in western Europe. In Byzantium the tradition of organ building seems to have continued unbroken after the Roman débâcle. The Byzantine emperor Constantinus Copronymus sent an organ to Pippin in 757 and in 812 an organ was brought by Byzantine visitors to Charlemagne's court at Aix-la-Chapelle[16]. Fourteen years later an organ was built there for Louis the Pious and the Emperor was proud to possess 'that organ of which Greece has been boasting more than of anything'[17]. Small bells were used in the western Christian Church from late Roman times as signals to call Christians to prayer. Later, monastic bells used in the liturgy were sometimes hung in the church roof, the bell-ringer standing between the sanctuary and the choir.

Secular instruments seem to have been simple horns for signalling hunts and royal and civic occasions, small lyres of the robust Celtic and Teutonic types for accompanying the chanting of epics and also as an adjunct to Christian missionary activity, fipple flutes, panpipes, small cylindrical and possibly conical reed pipes and perhaps bagpipes, all used in rustic or domestic contexts.

There is little accurate documentation of this period. All references to instrumental music are in Latin and use classical Latin terms – *cithara, lyra, tibia, fistula, tuba* – for instruments different from those to which the terms were originally applied. Many writers mixed reality with piety, symbolism and individual fancy when describing instruments. Iconographical evidence is scarce and there are few surviving instruments; fragments of Teutonic lyres have been found in Alemannic graves and enigmatic lyre or rudimentary harp fragments in the ship-burial at Sutton Hoo; in Ireland there are a few monastic bells. The nature of instruments and of instrumental practice during the first seven centuries of the Christian era is open both to research and to speculation.

1 See Sir C.L.Woolley, *Ur of the Chaldees*, 1950, *passim.*

2 G.Childe, *The Prehistory of European Society*, 1958, pp. 162–7.

3 C.Broholm, W.P.Larsen and G.Skjerne, *The Lurs of the Bronze Age*, 1949.

4 Buchner, op. cit., pl. 14.

5 I.Henderson, 'Ancient Greek Music', *The New Oxford History of Music*, i, 1957, pp. 376–8.

6 C.Sachs, op. cit., pp. 134–5.

7 See J.MacGillivray, 'The Cylindrical Reed Pipe from Antiquity to the 20th Century', *Music: Libraries and Instruments*, 1961, p. 218.

8 *Woodwind Instruments and their History*, 1962, p. 201.

9 A sample of his music is given in *Grove's Dictionary*, 5th ed., i, 1954, p. 264.

10 Baines, op. cit., p. 205; see also P.Collaer, 'Polyphonies de tradition populaire en Europe méditerranéenne', *Acta Musicologica*, xxxii, 1960, p. 51.

11 H.I.Marrou, *A History of Education in Antiquity*, 1956, p. 140.

12 J.E.Scott, 'Roman Music', *The New Oxford History of Music*, i, 1957, p. 405; A.Baines, *Bagpipes*, 1960, pp. 57–8.

13 W.Apel, 'Early History of the Organ', *Speculum*, xxiii, 1948, pp. 193–4.

14 Scott, op. cit., p. 416.

15 Sachs, op. cit., p. 120

16 Apel, op. cit., p. 204.

17 *Carmen de imagine Tetrici*, cited by Apel, op. cit., p. 205.

3 Christian institutions and Arab influences 900–1300

The Abbey of St Gall in Swabia benefited perhaps more than any other from the influx of monks from Ireland and Britain. Founded by an Irish monk early in the seventh century, it became about A.D. 800 the foremost monastery for the study of plainsong in Europe, and the first great centre for the production of liturgical manuscripts. This is the point in musical history at which the spread of Western musical notation began[1]. From about A.D. 1000 onwards illuminated manuscripts from *scriptoria* all over Europe are one of the main sources for our knowledge of musical instruments [35, 37–9, 41, etc]. Like the stone carvers [34, 46] and stained-glass artists, the illuminators by no means confined themselves to the instruments (real or symbolic) connected with Christian doctrine and liturgy, but ranged over most of the musical customs of their time. Manuscripts of secular song [49] contain a wealth of documentation in pictures, rarely with any symbolic or imaginary representations. Historical chronicles [51] and decorated objects for use [45] occasionally provide realistic depictions. While actual specimens surviving from before the sixteenth century are rare [36, 70], examples of the survival of medieval types among later folk instruments [42, 50, 53] help to fill this gap.

In spite of the comprehensive scope of the Christian iconography of musical instruments in the Middle Ages, the organ remained the only instrument used in the liturgy apart from exceptional occasions and customs. Descriptions, depictions and liturgical ordinals from the tenth century to the end of the twelfth indicate that the organ of that period (still hydraulic and with sliders) was so large an instrument that one has difficulty in imagining where it was placed in the church. An organ built at Winchester by Bishop Elphege (*d* 951) had four hundred pipes and two players, and is said to have needed the incredible number of seventy blowers. Depictions confirm that there were two players and that blowing was a strenuous task [35, 41]. The organ was associated particularly with one of the new forms of liturgical poetry of the time, the sequence at Mass on festivals[2]. The organist added to the joyful sound (the modern word 'accompany' is hardly appropriate) made by the choir and the bells, playing the plainsong melody probably with added parallel fifths above, in the manner of the contemporary vocal practice called *organum*. In the twelfth century choir-singers developed a festive style of two-part singing in which the soloist performed an elaborately decorative part against the plainsong. The chant was sung or perhaps played on a relatively small organ, which had its place with the singers on the screen between the choir and the nave [63, 76].

As musical educators, the cathedral and monastic song schools of the early Middle Ages needed instruments for demonstrating musical theory and for teaching singing.

The standard way of showing the connection between musical intervals and mathematical ratios was the monochord, a single string stretched over a wooden soundbox with a moveable bridge to divide the string [41]. Intervals and simple melodies could also be demonstrated with a set of tuned small bells (*cymbala*, frequently mistranslated as cymbals) [41, 44]. In the first half of the tenth century Odo, Abbot of Cluny, besides showing how to use a monochord[3], wrote instructions for setting the 'keys' on the instrument called *organistrum* (English hurdy-gurdy, French *simphonie*, *chifonie*). On this instrument the string or strings were rubbed by a rotating wheel and stopped by rods or bridges actuated by 'keys'. Although this rotary mechanical 'bow' may have appeared before the hand-operated bow (whose origin is still undiscovered), the earliest *organistrum* was clearly a mechanically sounded monochord, and not a precursor of the hand-bowed instruments. Odo does not say how many strings his *organistrum* had. Some twelfth-century depictions shows a large three-stringed instrument with two operators [44], and it is possible that melodies with *organum* in parallel fifths and octaves were played[4]. It is worth noting that each of these song school instruments in the product of some skilled process of manufacture.

For the monks trained in the Irish and Northumbrian schools the poetry of ancient Greece and Rome and the composition of secular verse were as normal a part of their training as were Christian doctrine and poetry. In this prolongation of the classical tradition it is reasonable to assume that the plucked strings, in their current forms, continued to be the accompanying instruments. This was probably the setting for the remarkable development of the frame harp, which ultimately ousted the Teutonic and Celtic lyre. To judge from the iconographical evidence, harp makers enormously increased the size of the soundbox, and ensured rigidity by giving the instrument a solid forepillar. This harp was a powerful instrument of large range, which no doubt called for professional skill to realize fully its musical capabilities [44, 46].

While the poet-singers of the epically-minded north used classical survivals and indigenous instruments, the troubadours and their attendant *joglars*, who created in the early twelfth century the first written poetry in a romance language, used many instruments of extra-European provenance. The three-string pear-shaped *lira* [42], which may have come from Byzantium, is already in the eleventh century depicted in conjunction with a bow. As the period of the troubadours of Provence passed into that of the *trouvères* of central and northern France, the *lira* was depicted with a definable neck and showed a trend from pear-shaped to oval, still with three strings [45].

Troubadour poetry itself is as a rule so little concerned with realistic things that it is a poor guide to its own setting; a rare exception is an anonymous *alba* (song of lovers at dawn):

> *Tro la gaita toque son caramel:*
> *Oi Deus, oi Deus, de l'alba! Tant tost ve!*[5]

Caramel is the French *calumel* or *chalemie*, the loud reed instrument of the watchman. A troubadour romance of the early thirteenth century, the late Provençal poem *Flamenca*, has a detailed description of the wedding-banquet at the château of Bourbon-L'Archambault of the count and the heroine Flamenca, in the presence of the King of France. This is something of a literary spectacular, for no less than fifteen hundred *joglars* are said to have been there:

> *L'uns viola lais de Cabrefoil,*
> *E l'autre cel de Tintagoil;*
> *L'us cantet cel dels Fins Amanz,*
> *E l'autre cel que fes Ivans.*
> *L'us menet arpa, l'autra viula;*
> *L'us flaütella, l'autre siula;*
> *L'uns mena giga, l'autre rota;*
> *L'us diz los motz e l'autrels nota;*
> *L'us estiva, l'autre flestella;*
> *L'us musa, l'autre caremella;*
> *L'us mandura e l'autre acorda*
> *Lo sauteri ab manicorda,*
> *L'us fai lo juec dels bavastelz,*
> *L'autre jugava de coutelz.*[6]

For the dancing afterwards:

> *.CC. juglar, bon viulador,*
> *S'i son acordat antre lor*
> *Que, dui e dui, de luein esteron*
> *Pels bancs, e la danza violeron*
> *Ques anc de point non i failliron.*[7]

One cannot be certain of the precise interpretation of all the joglars' instruments in this list. *Viola* and *violeron* (verbs), *viula* and *viulador* (nouns) refer to the fiddle. (This term is a generic word for bowed strings; viol, though often used for fiddle in this period, belongs in modern terminology to the family of fretted bowed strings of the sixteenth and seventeenth centuries.) *Flaütella, flestella,* and probably *siula,* are fipple flutes; *giga* is very likely a small fiddle, or very possibly a bowed lyre; *rota* is perhaps a lyre; *estiva, musa* and *caremella* are reed instruments, mouth-blown or bagged. The heroic tales of the Lay of the Honeysuckle, of Tintagel and of the Faithful Lovers, and 'the lay that Ivan made', were sung, and the dances danced, to the bowed string instrument.

While the historical antecedents of the bowed string instruments are still mysterious, the mandora and the psaltery have known Arab predecessors. The mandora of the early thirteenth century was a small fingerboard instrument, probably derived from the Arab *rebab* but played with a plectrum. The psaltery was the Western form of the instrumental type whose generic name is zither, in which strings are placed horizontally over a sound-box. European psalteries were sometimes rectangular [44] or trapezoid [48] in form; the characteristic shape was pig's-head [49, 61, 62, 73], later called *istromento di porco*[8]. The Arab form, *kanun* [40], which still survives, is played with plectra attached to the fingers; medieval Western psalteries were played with goose-quill plectra or the fingertips.

The Saracens had highly developed military music on shawms, trumpets and drums whose sounds, stimulating to their own troops and frightening to their enemy's, certainly made a powerful impression on the Crusaders. In the West trumpets seem to have been used initially only as heralding instruments by royalty and high aristocracy [51]. Already in the thirteenth century drums sometimes had snares – strings of gut or wire stretched across the head, which add sharpness to the sound [49].

By the second half of the thirteenth century this procession of new instruments, whose sound must have made an exciting impact when first heard by European ears, had become settled members of the Western musical community. The bagpipe, which in the Graeco-Roman world had been the instrument of mendicants, may have survived into the early medieval West, but is not certainly recorded until the twelfth century[9]. From then on it is depicted and spoken of as an instrument of shepherds, angels, joglars and minnesingers (the German inheritors of the *trouvère* tradition) [49]. From about the same time the fipple flute becomes almost equally ubiquitous.

The written music of the Middle Ages, whether sacred or secular, very rarely indicated the instrument on which an instrumental piece or the interludes in a song should be played. A possible exception is a motet without words with the title *In saeculum viellatoris* ('fiddle-player's piece on the tenor *In saeculum*') in a manuscript of the second half of the thirteenth century[10]. As a rule, however, the choice was the performer's, made in the light of social conventions, distinctions of musical style and intimate knowledge of the characters and capacities of instruments, all in a complex pattern which we today are far from having reconstructed. The motet was the newest genre of written part-music in the thirteenth century. One, two or three vocal parts were composed against a known tune, either from plainsong or *trouvère* song, which was played on an instrument – this part was called the 'tenor' because it held to the known tune. Sacred motets were sung in church, and the tenor would probably have been played on the positive organ on the screen. Both sacred and secular motets, including those with sacred Latin words in one part and secular French words in another, as well as late *trouvère* part-music, were sung for recreation by learned clergy and lay *cognoscenti* (John of Grocheo, writing about 1300, said that motets should not be performed for ordinary people, who would not appreciate their subtlety and therefore would not enjoy them, but only for cultured people who look out for the subtle points in art)[11]. In this case the tenor was probably played on a portative organ [66] or on the large five-string fiddle which is depicted from the early thirteenth century onwards [49], often with an off-the-fingerboard drone string[12]. This instrument, with its big body and long bow, clearly had the bigger tone needed for sustained part-playing; the smaller three-string fiddle must have been quite inadequate for this purpose.

The lavishly illustrated manuscripts of *Las Cántigas de Santa Maria*, whose texts were written by Alfonso the Wise before his accession to the throne of Castile and León in 1252, have often been considered the most comprehensive iconographical source for instruments of the second half of the thirteenth century. They are certainly later in date than the poems, probably later than the music and in all likelihood date from after, rather than before, 1300. In any case, the wealth of instrumental types – pipe and tabor, transverse flute, bladder pipe, bagpipe, Moorish lute, rebab, kanun, trumpet, drums and so on – cannot be taken as representing widespread musical practice of the time. It is, rather, a rich instrumental confluence from many places, with a strong Mediterranean emphasis.

1 For the extant musical documents of Greece see I.Henderson, op. cit., pp. 363–76. There are no Roman remains of music.

2 F.Ll.Harrison, *Music in Medieval Britain*, 1958, pp. 205–6.

3 In the *Enchiridion musices*, c 935; translation in O.Strunk, *Source Readings in Music History*, 1950, pp. 103–9.

4 See H.Panum, *The Stringed Instruments of the Middle Ages*, 1940, pp. 293–300.

5 A.Pillet and H.Carstens, *Bibliographie des troubadours*, 1933, poet 461, poem 113, cited in H.Davenson, *Les Troubadours*, 1961, p. 100.

6 *The Romance of Flamenca*, ed. M.E.Porter, 1962, lines 600 ff.; this edition has a free English verse translation.

7 Ibid., lines 728–32.

8 According to Michael Praetorius in the *Syntagma* (1619).

9 A.Baines, *Bagpipes*, 1960, pp. 63–8.

10 Ed. P.Aubry in *Cent motets du XIIIe siècle*, 3 vols., 1908, p. 226.

11 E.Rohloff, *Der Musiktraktat des Johannes de Grocheo*, 1943, p. 56.

12 See F.Ll.Harrison, 'Tradition and Innovation in Instrumental Usage, 1100–1450' in *Aspects of Medieval and Renaissance Music*, 1964.

4 Dispersal and specialization

1300–1500

When medieval writers on musical theory mentioned instruments they usually confined their remarks to the instruments used for teaching and for setting pitch for singers, namely small bells, organ and monochord. John of Grocheo is a rare case of one who described, though briefly, the whole musical scene of his day. These are some of the things he had to say about instruments, writing particularly about music in Paris:

> Some people classify instruments according to their method of sound-production. Hence they say that sound is produced either by blowing, as in the trumpet [*tuba*], shawm [*calamus*], flute [*fistula*] and organ [*organa*], or by striking, as in strings, drum [*typanum*], and small and large bells [*cymbalum, campana*]. Here I propose to remark on the nature and typology of instruments only in relation to the various musical possibilities to which they give rise. In the foremost category are string instruments, such as psaltery, harp [*cithara*], *lira* [*lyra*], lute [or perhaps guitar; his term is *quitarra sarracenica*], and fiddle [*viella*]. Distinctions of pitch on these instruments are finer and more subtle because they have strings which can be shortened and lengthened at will.
>
> The fiddle is superior to all the string instruments we have mentioned. . . . Although some other instruments may move the minds of men more powerfully by their sound – for example the drum and trumpet when played in banquets, jousts and tournaments – nevertheless all kinds of music are more sensitively realized on the fiddle.
>
> A good artist introduces every song or dance tune, and every kind of music generally, on a fiddle. Only three kinds of music are commonly played at the banquets and entertainments of rich men, namely, lyric songs [*cantus coronatus*], and shorter and longer dance tunes [*ductia et stantipes*][1].

Grocheo explains two paragraphs later that a *ductia* is a dance tune with three or four strains, a *stantipes* one with four to seven strains. It is safe to assume that the fiddle whose powers of expression he so admired was the large five-string kind.

In the late fourteenth century drum and wind ensembles of various kinds began to be used in the newly organized professional armies of Europe. The prototypes of the drums were Arabian or Turkish. The very small kettle-drums called nakers (Arabic *naqqara*) played with the fingers [64] were the first to come to the West, where they were known by about A.D. 1300. By the end of the fourteenth century pairs of large kettle-drums [67a] were being played with trumpets in outdoor ceremonial music. From the fifteenth century onwards mounted kettle-drummers and trumpeters were used in military and

aristocratic contexts; in the army this combination remained for centuries the pre-
rogative of cavalry regiments. The combination of the long cylindrical drum [65] with
the transverse flute, the latter instrument now definitely documented in the medieval
West (it is well depicted in the *Book of Hours* of Jeanne d'Evreux of *c* 1320[2] [64] and mentioned
as *traversayne* in Eustache Deschamps's lament for Machaut[3], who died in 1377), was a
speciality of German mercenaries as the music of infantry. As the fife and drum band it
has remained infantry music up to our own day. An Italian painting of the first half of
the fifteenth century shows pikemen at the capture of Pisa in 1406 being led by a boy
with pipe and tabor – the minimal form of military band [105]. The pairing of three-hole
fipple flute with small snare drum beaten by the same player [54, 56] is often found in
quite another context, as the music of unsophisticated dances like the round dance
(*carole*) [56]. In the earliest stage of its western European history the *carole* was a danced
song for group with leader[4]. In the fourteenth century it is depicted with music played
by instruments: bagpipe, pipe and tabor, shawms [56, 60]. In at least one case the paired
shawms are of different sizes [60], and therefore connote part-playing in some form.
Less realistic, perhaps, is the image of a heavenly *carole* with music on a soft plucked
instrument, the gittern [59], predecessor of the flat-backed guitar. With the imported
Eastern drums came other percussion instruments like the flat cymbals [65, 67c], and the
triangle, with or without jingles [67d, 77].

When Chaucer finished *Troilus and Criseyde* he gave it to the world with these words:

> And red wher so thow be, or elles songe,
> That thow be understonde, God I beseche.

By Chaucer's time the vast repertory of the romances had ceased to be a flourishing
oral tradition, and the stories were more often read aloud or in private than retold to
the music of the fiddle. From about the middle of the fourteenth century onwards the
minstrels who played for royalty and aristocracy were likely to be household staff, and
their music to be part of a recurrent pattern of court and household events. Particular
instruments tended to be used for particular kinds of function, and the social distinctions
between them tended to be more sharply drawn. Trumpets were for heraldry in peace
and war [72], and for occasions of high ceremonial like tournaments [57, 58] and triumphal
entries. Although 'minstrel' was sometimes used in a general sense of all professional
instrumentalists, ceremonial and personal trumpeters were a separate group and were
paid higher rates. In 1379 John of Gaunt, Duke of Lancaster, signed a contract with John

Buckingham, clarioner, to attend him for life. Buckingham was to eat at the minstrels' table and have as wages sevenpence-halfpenny a day in peacetime when at court, twelve pence when away from court in the Duke's service, and as fees five pounds a year in peacetime and ten pounds a year in wartime. John of Gaunt also had two 'trumpours' and eight minstrels. At Kenilworth at New Year in 1380 there were, besides these household men, the herald and four minstrels of the Earl of Cambridge, the herald and eleven minstrels of the Earl of Nottingham, three minstrels of Sir Baldwin Freville and one freelance minstrel. All had money from the Duke, the heralds twenty shillings each, the minstrels six shillings and eightpence each[5].

During the fourteenth century the terms *haut* (loud) and *bas* (soft) began to be used as a basic classification of instruments. They became familiar to clerks and poets, as well as to musicians. A patent by Charles VI of France in 1407 to the guild of Paris musicians refers to them as '*Ménestriers, joueurs d'instruments tant haulx comme bas*'[6].

The loud instruments comprised trumpets, drums and cymbals, bagpipe and shawm, and hunting horn; the soft instruments were strings, now including the lute, which came to the West rather later than the other instruments of Arab derivation, flutes both fipple and transverse, and portative organ. Of medieval soft reed instruments practically nothing is known apart from the name of one – *douçaine* or *dulzaina*. Music for aristocratic processions [72] and ceremonial banquets [80] was played by shawms with a low trumpet or draw-trumpet. The shawm was a double-reed-on-conical-tube instrument of great loudness and power. The player supported his lips against a pirouette at the end of the instrument, and the large reed vibrated inside his mouth – as that of the Oriental shawm-like instruments does today. The draw-trumpet was drawn telescopically on a fixed mouthpipe, a crude way of increasing the melodic possibilities of the trumpet. Any natural trumpet (i.e., one without valves) can play only notes of the harmonic series, which has large gaps in the lower register and provides a continuous scale only in the upper register. The lower-pitched trumpet of the later Middle Ages had its greater length made first roughly S-shaped [71], and finally folded into the now familiar shape [75a]. The high draw-trumpet cannot have been an efficient instrument, and has little traceable history. The draw form of low trumpet, however, seems to have been successful from the start, and developed during the fifteenth century into the sackbut, identical in all essentials with the modern trombone.

Although numbers of unattached minstrels still freelanced at fairs, on pilgrimages, and wherever there were chances of reward, the rise of urban life in the fourteenth century saw many minstrels resident in cities organizing themselves into fraternities with city and church affiliations, in order to regulate their professional appearances at civic and guild banquets, in church processions, and on the social occasions of the citizens. The soft instruments had their place in the music-making of urban people, as well as in the more intimate moments of court life. Particularly in northern Italy the musical life of cities gave rise to the writing of secular part-music for voices with and without instruments by such composers as Giovanni of Florence, Jacopo of Bologna, Bartolino of Padua, and, most famous of all, Francesco Landini (*d* 1397). In France the milieu of secular part-music was the church/court axis, in which the greatest French poet-composer of the age, Guillaume de Machaut, lived and wrote. This is the first important era of secular part-music; of Landini alone there survive 154 pieces, all secular[7]. Machaut considered that the harp surpassed all other soft instruments[8]; in its various forms it was certainly widely useful [68, 76, 82*a*, 83][9]. Landini is more than once depicted with a portative organ [66], and his playing of it is said to have charmed the birds into silence[10]. According to Chaucer's Pardoner the plucked string instruments did not always keep the best company:

> In Flaunders whilom was a companye
> Of yonge folkes, that hauntede folye
> As ryot, hasard, stywes and tavernes
> Wher as, with lutes, harpes and gyternes
> They daunce, and play at dees, both day and night.

The small lute, plectrum-plucked and comparable with the modern mandolin rather than with the big Renaissance lute, was particularly associated with popular entertainers [81]. Not so the fipple flute, as Eustache Deschamps tells us:

> *Car princes oyent voluntiers*
> *Le flajol.*[11]

John of Gaunt had a 'fistula nomine Ricordo' – this is the earliest known occurrence of the name recorder (in the sense of 'keepsake'). His wife Blanche sang to the harp (*cithara*), and their son, who made himself Henry IV of England in 1399, owned a harp. He probably played it well, for he was the accomplished composer of music for his own chapel[12].

In the fifteenth century secular part-music for voices and instruments was a flourishing form of composition in France, Italy, Germany and the Netherlands, though not yet in England. While the twilight of the Middle Ages was illuminated by the brilliant court of Philip the Good of Burgundy (*d* 1467), where Gilles Binchois and Guillaume Dufay served as composers, the Renaissance merchant classes of Philip's French and Flemish dominions and of the new commercial centres of the Netherlands were beginning to practise the courtly arts. For this growing amateur public composers like Jacob Obrecht (1450–1505) set poetry in French, Dutch and Italian to music which was rhythmically and melodically less subtle than that of Binchois and Dufay, and therefore less demanding in ensemble. The first part-music ever printed (Petrucci's *Odhecaton*, Venice, 1501), was music of this vocal-instrumental genre by Obrecht, Josquin des Prés and many other composers[13].

Some of the new developments in instruments in the last part of the fifteenth century clearly reflect the rise of the first large amateur musical public, while others appear to have resulted from changing professional aims and practices. By the end of the century the rebec had evolved [84], having absorbed certain features both of the Arab *rebab* and of the old pear-shaped *lira*. A specialized fiddle form with off-the-fingerboard drone strings – a survival of drone strings on the earlier fiddles – was the *lira da braccio* [82, 85, 98, 109]. *Da braccio* means 'of the arm' as distinct from *da gamba* ('of the leg'), the playing position of the new viols [89d, 98]. The viol family is a peculiar excursus in the long history of European bowed strings. Made in sizes ranging from small treble to (ultimately) large bass, these had the flat back of the guitar, generally five or six strings, and frets, i.e., pieces of gut tied around the neck which give a predetermined stopping point for the string. This last device, which absolves the player from the responsibility of determining minutely his own finger positions – as he must on an instrument without frets – had long been in use on lutes [87] and guitars. The bass of the family was a useful member in its own right, and remained so until the eighteenth century. It is possible that the family as a whole was developed for amateur performance of instrumental and vocal-instrumental part-music; an analogous development took place with the recorder. Both families are characterized by a relatively narrow dynamic range and a detached and unemotional quality of sound.

An event of lasting importance in this period was the replacing of the positive [63] by the large church organ [79] on the screen or in the organ-gallery of larger churches, the positive continuing to have useful functions as a chamber organ [76, 77]. Another happening of cardinal importance was the birth of the keyed strings, the clavichord and harpsichord [77]. In the former the strings are struck by a brass blade ('tangent') fixed to the inner end of the key; in the latter they are plucked by a quill framed in a 'jack' which is pushed upward by the inner end of the key. It is likely that the clavichord, at any rate, was known in the fourteenth century. Both instruments are documented by the fourteen-thirties, notably in an account of their construction by Henry Arnaut, sometime physician and astrologer to Philip the Good[14]. While one of the functions of the larger organ was to alternate with a choir, and some music is directly intended for this, a good deal of secular music was played on the organ in the fifteenth century, especially in Germany, and the other keyboards were auxiliary or alternative to it. The weight of evidence suggests that they were developed in church circles as convenient rehearsal substitutes for the organ. By the end of the fifteenth century the lute had been greatly enlarged into the finger-plucked form for polyphonic playing [87] in which it is now generally remembered and in which it has been revived. Intricate plectrum techniques can still be heard, however, on the Rumanian *cobza,* the Balkan *tamburitza* and the Greek *bouzouki.* The vibrant and energetic sound of these popular lutes suggests something of what was lost when the European lute was developed into a part-playing instrument.

1 Ed. cit., p. 52.

2 See E.Winternitz, 'Bagpipes for the Lord', *Bulletin of the Metropolitan Museum of Art,* xvi, 1958, p. 279.

3 Set to music by F.Andrieu; modern edition by F.Ludwig, *Guillaume de Machaut, Musikalische Werke,* i, 1926, p. 49.

4 See R.L.Greene, *A Selection of English Carols,* 1962, pp. 2–11.

5 Ed. E.C.Lodge and R.Somerville, *John of Gaunt's Register, 1379–1383,* i, 1937, pp. 15, 49, 113.

6 Cited in E.Bowles, 'Haut and Bas: the grouping of musical instruments in the Middle Ages', *Musica Disciplina,* viii, 1954, p. 119.

7 Ed. L.Schrade, *Polyphonic Music of the Fourteenth Century,* iv, 1958.

8 Quoted from *Dit de la harpe* in F.Dick, 'Bezeichnungen für Saiten- und Schlaginstrumente in der altfranzösischen Literatur', *Giessener Beiträge zur Romanischen Philologie,* xxv, 1932, p. 26.

9 See J.Rimmer, 'James Talbot's Manuscript: VI. Harps', *Galpin Society Journal,* xvi, 1963, p. 63, and 'The Morphology of the Irish Harp', *Galpin Society Journal,* xvii, 1964, p. 39.

10 L.Ellinwood, 'The Fourteenth Century in Italy', *New Oxford History of Music,* iii, 1960, p. 36.

11 *Du métier profitable,* cited Bowles, op. cit., p. 126 from *Œuvres complètes,* ed. A.Queux de St Hilaire, vi, 1889, p. 128.

12 F.Ll.Harrison, *Music in Medieval Britain,* 1958, p. 221.

13 *Harmonice Musices Odhecaton A,* ed. H.Hewitt, 1942.

14 Ed. G.le Cerf and E.-R.Lebande, *Les Traités d'Henri-Arnault de Zwolle et de divers anonymes,* 1932.

5 Consorts and contrasts 1500–1610

During the first half of the sixteenth century the panoply of court life in Europe reached new levels of luxury and ostentation. The Holy Roman Emperors Maximilian I (1493–1519) and Charles V (1519–58) set standards of magnificence which many courts emulated, but none could equal [89]. In the procession at Charles V's coronation by Pope Clement VII in Bologna '*marchoient en grande nombre les trompettes et clairons, les cornets et buccines*'[1]. *Clairon*, which formerly meant a short trumpet, now referred to exclusively high-register playing (later called *clarin* in Germany) in contrast to the less exacting low-register playing of the field-trumpeters; *buccines* are trombones. At the famous rendezvous at the Field of the Cloth of Gold in 1520 Henry VIII and Wolsey were preceded by five hundred guards, two thousand infantry, archers, gentlemen and trumpeters. Francis I's cortège was led by a hundred Swiss pikemen accompanied by their '*joueurs de flûte et de tambour*'. The two great processions faced each other for a moment of pregnant silence; then all at once there sounded fanfares of 'Trumpettes, Sagbuttes and all other Minstrelles on both sides'[2]. In the same year the procession following Charles V's coronation at Aix-la-Chapelle as the fiftieth possessor of the throne of Charlemagne was led by twelve trumpeters and eight heralds[3]. When the Emperor paid his state visit to England two years later he brought with him his complete 'Grande chapelle' with singers, organist and blower, eight trumpeters, a drummer ('Broully tamburin'), three herald-trumpeters and six flute-players (*phiffers*)[4]. At Henry VIII's death in 1547 his household establishment included eighteen trumpeters, seven 'mynstrells', eight 'musytyans' all named Bassani, four 'shackebuttes', six 'vyolls' (? violins) all Italians, five 'fluttes', two 'vialls', a 'fyfer' and a drummer, a harper and a bagpiper[5].

Throughout the century the ducal courts of Germany and Austria maintained large establishments of singers and players, who performed in both sacred and secular music. One of the most ardent of musical patrons was Albert V of Bavaria, whose court was at Munich. The music at the banquet celebrating his marriage to Renée of Lorraine in 1568 began with Annibale Padovano's *Battaglia*[6] (the battle-piece was a favourite type, first vocal and later instrumental) played by cornetts [67j, 91, 113, 114] and trombones. With the first course five high cornetts (*cornetti alti*) and two trombones played a motet by Roland de Lassus, director of music at the court and the most celebrated composer in Europe. For the second course eight trombones ('the bass one going an octave lower than the others') played a madrigal by Alessandro Striggio. With the fish there was a six-part motet by Cipriano da Rore played by *viole da brazzo*. With the roast another piece by Padovano, apparently for two six-part choirs of instruments or voices, was performed

by six *viole da brazzo*, a cornett with five trombones, and a '*regale dolce*' (soft reed organ)
which probably played with the strings. With the fifth course there was a piece for three
choirs, played by six low viols ('a fourth lower than usual'), six recorders (*flauti*) and six
voices with a harpsichord. The music with the sixth course was played by a completely
heterogeneous ensemble of – in the order of the contemporary account – harpsichord,
trombone, recorder, lute, *cornamusa*, mute cornett (*cornetto muto*, a straight cornett with
built-in mouthpiece), viol and small shawm (*piffero*). For the seventh and last course a
piece for three choirs was performed by two homogeneous groups, one of four viols and
the other of four large recorders, and a heterogeneous group made up of *dolzaina*, *cornamusa*, shawm and mute cornett. The *cornamusa* and *dolzaina* were reed instruments of which
no specimens have survived. The grand finale was performed by the whole *capella* – this
term, like *Kapelle* in German, meant the total musical establishment. It was an eight-
part work first played by eight viols, eight *viole da braccio*, and a mixed ensemble of *fagotto*
(bassoon predecessor), *cornamusa*, mute cornett, high cornett, low cornett (*cornetto grosso
storto* – the largest cornetts have a double curve), shawm, *dolzaina* and large trombone,
and then sung by 'eight sonorous voices'[7].

The remarkable thing about this succession of pieces, viewed as a musical programme,
is the way it shows off in progressive order the full range of instrumental possibilities:
first homogeneous groups (called in England 'whole consorts'), then the setting of whole
consorts against mixed groups ('broken consorts'), then a large broken consort, and at
the last (leaving a final Moresca out of account) a complete *tutti*, with instruments of
different kinds playing the same parts in unison. Though we have no detailed record of
the practice of instrumentation in this period, it was clearly not haphazard, but took
into account such factors as the style of the music, the sonorities and capabilities of the
instruments, and the acoustics of the place of performance. If this were out of doors, the
weather was a consideration. In 1569 François Robillard of Paris, 'master player of instruments', contracted with a group of hatters (*chappliers*) to provide ten musicians for their
festivities on the feast of St Michael; they would play six *aubades* on cornetts (*cornetz à boucquin*)
and violins if it did not rain, or on flutes (*fleutes d'alemens*) and trombone (*saqueboutte*) if it did[8].

The making of certain instruments in a range of sizes corresponding in a general way
with the parts of a vocal ensemble was a radically new thing in this period. Flutes, which
were used much more widely than before [90, 98, 105c, 112] were made in at least the basic
three sizes of treble, tenor and bass; recorders [91, 92a, 99], viols [89d, 103, 112] and cromornes [89c, 92c] were made in a range wide enough to provide a whole consort of each

family. The cromorne (German *Krummhorn*) was a curved wind instrument with cylindrical bore and double reed enclosed in a windcap; it was probably derived from a central European folk instrument[9]. Ensembles of cornetts generally had trombones playing the lower parts. The earlier use of mixed instrumental groups, now in the form of broken consorts, continued on a grander scale and with a greater variety of instruments than before, including, in the latter part of the sixteenth century, soft-toned double-reed instruments like the racketts and fagotts.

One of the points to be taken into account, especially by amateurs, in planning a broken consort was intonation, as we hear from Hercole Bottrigari, a learned amateur of music, mathematics and classics, in his *Il Desiderio* of 1594[10]. Classifying instruments from the point of view of tuning as stable (organ, harpsichord, harp), stable but alterable (viol, lute, recorder, flute, cornett) and entirely alterable (trombone, *lira*, *ribechini*, that is, bowed strings without frets), he advises mixing any two classes, since players of both stable-alterable and entirely alterable instruments can adjust their intonation to that of the stable instruments, but not mixing all three, since that will produce 'a real *concerto*, or "battle" of instruments, instead of a *concento*, a word which means the union and concord of voices and of diverse sounds'. Bottrigari was probably addressing this recommendation to the members of the Italian academies, where amateurs and professionals were involved on equal terms. According to him the best instrumental concerts were at Venice, at the *Accademia Filarmonico* in Verona, and at the court of Alfonso II, Duke of Ferrara, where Bottrigari lived for some time. The Duke's singers doubled on instruments and were excellent players. The Duke was evidently one of the first admirers of old instruments, keeping a collection 'because of their forms being different from those in which they are usually made today'. He also possessed the marvellous experimental *arcicembalo* ('arch-harpsichord') invented by Nicola Vicentino, *maestro di cappella* to Duke Ercole d'Este in 1546–9, which had six manuals to demonstrate the theoretical tunings of Greek antiquity. (The Bologna Conservatory has today a similarly experimental *arcicembalo* made in 1606 by Vito Trasuntino of Venice[11].) Because of the care given to the instruments and the meticulous preparation of the music, Bottrigari excepts the Duke's concerts from his reservations about mixing types of instruments, observing that 'none of those who try to make similar concerts follow the example of close concord and of unanimity attained by these excellent musicians of Ferrara in their *gran Concerto*'. The matching of intonation is not, of course, a peculiarly sixteenth-century problem, but one ever present in ensemble playing.

In the second half of the century in the courts of northern Italy instruments were coming to be used in theatrical entertainments connected with state occasions. At the celebrations following the marriage of Ferdinando de' Medici and Christine of Lorraine in Florence in 1589, the *sinfonia* which accompanied the opening of the heavens in the first *intermedio* – a short diversion with music done between the acts of a play – was performed by three small and three large lutes, a psaltery, three tenor viols and a bass viol, four trombones, a cornett, a flute (*traversa*), a cittern (*cetera*), a mandola and a small violin, here called *sopranino di viola* [120], played 'with the greatest accomplishment' by Alessandro Striggio[12]. This sort of 'orchestra' is the historical background to the instrumentation in Monteverdi's *Orfeo* (the mythical poet-musician was a favourite subject in the academies), the first masterwork in the form of opera, which was staged at the *Accademia degli Invaghiti* in Mantua, and shortly after at the theatre of the Duke, whose *maestro di cappella* Monteverdi was. Here another criterion, that of association, affected the choice and use of instruments, though this had constantly been implicit in their social function. Trumpets and kettle-drums announce the opening of the opera with the customary thrice-repeated fanfare-toccata (the English 'tucket')[13]; the keyboard instrument accompanying the dialogue is harpsichord, organ with wood pipes, or regal according to the dramatic situation; the recorder is associated with pastoral scenes, cornetts and trombones with the solemnity of the underworld.

In the bowed-string section of his orchestra Monteverdi used two small violins, four normal violins, two cellos, three bass viols and two double-bass viols; it is clear that in Italy the 'violin family' was already firmly established. Precisely where the almost miraculously perfect form of the violin was devised is not clear, but it is certain that the most substantial early contribution was made by Italian makers, notably Andrea Amati in Cremona [108], first of an eminent family in a place later made famous by Stradivari, and Gaspar da Salò (1540–1609) in Brescia. In the violin certain features of the rebec, the medieval fiddle and the *lira da braccio* were incorporated. An instrument primarily for professionals, at whatever social level, its great range of expression and vitality of tone were among the marked advantages which enabled it eventually to oust every other bowed-string instrument.

The instruments most played by amateurs were the recorder [99], the fretted strings – including viol, lute (in Spain *vihuela da mano* [94], flat-backed like a guitar but tuned like a lute), cittern and bandora [111, 112] – and in affluent circles the keyboard instruments, including harpsichord [100], clavichord [101, 102], virginal [106], chamber organ, regal and the combination of organ and harpsichord [107, 116]. The cittern and bandora, almost exclusively amateur affairs, were mainly chord-playing instruments; both were wire-strung, whereas the viols and the lute were gut-strung. A good indication of amateur interest is the printing of elementary instruction-books. Silvestro Ganassi brought out the first method for the recorder in Venice in 1535 [91] and later did one for viols. Petrucci printed a series of lute-music books in the decade following the *Odhecaton*. Pierre Attaignant began a similar series in Paris in 1529 with an introduction to lute-playing. Lute-players in England had two translations (1568, 1574) of an instruction-book by the French publisher and lutenist Adrien le Roy. In Germany the aim was towards school education. Though an excellent example of the educational book on instruments, Virdung's *Musica getutscht* of 1511 perpetuated supposed biblical instruments from medieval writers, nonsenses which were still taken seriously in the eighteenth century. Luis Milan's *El Maestro* (Valencia, 1536) is arranged progressively for beginners on the vihuela, while Tomas de Sancta Maria's *Libro . . . de tañer fantasia* (Valladolid, 1565) gives special attention to playing the clavichord and to the techniques of improvising which the well-trained amateur was expected to master. In England there was a printed tutor for the lute, bandora and orpharion, this last an adaptation of the bandora with the tuning and playing technique of the lute (William Barley's *New Booke of Tabliture*, 1596), and also one for the cittern (Anthony Holborne's *Cittharn School*, 1597).

The role of instruments in churches varied between the extremes of total exclusion from Calvinist churches, as part of their attempt to return to a primitive Christianity, and full acceptance of appropriate types in the Catholic churches of the Empire and the south [114]. Each of the important Spanish cathedrals gave full-time engagements to six or eight players of shawms, cornetts, flutes and sackbuts[14] as well as an organist and harpist. In France, however, instruments were not used in church services until towards the end of the century. In pre-Reformation England every parish church of any size had an organ, and the best composers for the instrument created the idiomatically brilliant keyboard style which was the foundation for the later virginalists. Edward VI ordered screens and organs to be destroyed, and many were. Though Elizabeth I avoided enforcing a ban, there was no effective revival until after the accession of James I (1603), when not only organs but cornetts and sackbuts began to be the normal concomitants of cathedral music.

One of the earliest pieces of ensemble music for which the composer indicated the precise instrumentation was Giovanni Gabrieli's *Sonata pian' e forte* (1597) for two instrumental choirs, one of a cornett and three trombones, the other a lower-pitched group of a viola (which he calls *violino*) and three trombones[15]. It is interesting that this is also the earliest ensemble work to have indications of dynamic levels, as its name implies. Two years later Thomas Morley published his *First Book of Consort Lessons*[16] for a broken consort, a popular one at the time, of treble viol (or violin), flute of alto range, bass viol, lute, cittern and bandora [112]. In publications of solo instrumental music alternatives were commonly given, as for example in Antonio de Cabezon's *Obras de musica para tecla* [=keyboard], *arpa y vihuela* (Madrid, 1578). Though a good deal of specifically keyboard music was produced, particularly in Italy and England, interchange was rife, with choral music, sacred and secular, and dance music being transcribed for lute, harpsichord and organ.

In 1610 Monteverdi printed his *Vespers* with indications of instruments. In the second book of *Sacrae Symphoniae* (posthumous, 1615), Gabrieli did the same, though not consistently, for the great vocal-instrumental ensembles for which St Mark's, with its separate gallery for each group of performers, was so renowned. The English traveller Thomas Coryat wrote about his ravishment and stupefaction on hearing the services at St Mark's in 1608:

.... Sometimes there sang sixteene or twenty men together, having their master or moderator to keepe them in order; and when they sung, the instrumentall musitians played also. Sometimes sixteene played together upon their instruments, ten Sagbuts, foure Cornets, and two Violdegambaes of an extraordinary greatness; sometimes tenne, sixe Sagbuts and foure Cornets; sometimes two, a Cornet and a treble violl. Of those treble viols I heard three severall there, whereof each was so good, especially one that I observed above the rest, that I never heard the like before. Those that played upon the treble viols, sung and played together, and sometimes two singular fellowes played together upon Theorboes, to which they sung also, who yeelded admirable sweet musicke, but so still that they could scarce be heard but by those that were very neare them. These two Theorbists concluded that nights musicke, which continued three whole howers at the least. For they beganne about five of the clocke, and ended not before eight. Also it continued as long in the morning: at every time that every severall musicke played, the Organs, whereof there are seven faire paire in that room, standing al in a row together, plaied with them[17].

1 *Fêtes et cérémonies au temps de Charles Quint*, ed. J.Jacquot, 1960, p. 40.

2 Ibid., pp. 120–1.

3 Ibid., p. 167.

4 Ed. W.Jerdan, *Rutland Papers*, 1842, pp. 60, 64–5.

5 H.C. de Lafontaine, *The King's Musick*, 1909, pp. 7–8.

6 Printed in *Istituzione e Monumenti dell'Arte Musicale Italiana*, i, ed. G. Benvenuti, 1931, p. 177.

7 *Dialoghi di Massimo Troiano*, Venice, 1569, pp. 60 ff.

8 F.Lesure, 'La facture instrumentale à Paris au seizième siècle', *Galpin Society Journal*, vii, 1954, p. 28.

9 A.Baines, *Woodwind Instruments and their History*, 1962, pp. 252–6.

10 Facsimile ed. K.Mayer, 1924; English translation by C.MacClintock, 1962.

11 See R.Russell, *The Harpsichord and Clavichord*, 1959, pl. 13.

12 E.Vogel, *Bibliothek der gedruckten weltlichen Vocalmusik Italiens*, i, 1962, pp. 383–4.

13 See C.Titcomb, 'Baroque Court and Military Trumpets and Kettledrums', *Galpin Society Journal*, ix, 1956, p. 69.

14 R.Stevenson, *Spanish Cathedral Music in the Golden Age*, 1961, p. 298.

15 Printed in *Historical Anthology of Music*, ed. A.T.Davison and W.Apel, i, 1954, No. 173.

16 Ed. S.Beck, 1959.

17 *Galpin Society Journal*, i, 1948, p. 27, from *Coryat's Crudities*, 1611, p. 252.

6 National diversities and Baroque splendours 1610–1750

The style of large-scale instrumental and vocal-instrumental music which so impressed Coryat at St Mark's was carried to its final stage by Roman composers, of whom the best-known is Orazio Benevoli. Commissioned to compose a Mass for the dedication of Salzburg Cathedral in 1628, Benevoli wrote a work in fifty-three parts – not 'real' parts since there was much doubling – disposed in two eight-part choirs, two string ensembles, one group of woodwind and three of brass instruments[1]. While ensemble music in the sixteenth century had called as a rule for an equal weight of tone in each part, the ensemble style of the seventeenth century was based on the predominance of the highest part or pair of parts, with a balancing weight of tone in the bass, and a relatively light filling-in accompaniment, improvised on a chord-playing instrument. Each of the choirs in Benevoli's work had a supporting accompaniment, and the coherence of the whole great ensemble was ensured by a master accompanist. The improviser of an accompaniment in Baroque music played from a bass part with figures below, the technical term for which was *basso continuo* (in England 'thorough bass', later 'figured bass') [137]. The figures were a shorthand for the required chords, which were more or less elaborated at the player's discretion.

In Venice after Gabrieli's time large ensembles went out of fashion, as Heinrich Schütz reported after his second stay there in 1628–9; his first had been as a pupil of Gabrieli in 1609–12. The vogue was now for small media, such as solo voice and continuo, called monodies, or a small group of solo voices with one or more instruments and continuo. Many large instruments capable of playing continuo bass were developed at the turn of the sixteenth century. Among them were the great harps, including the triple harp [123a], the *lirone*, which was a chord-playing bass form of the *lira da braccio*, and big lutes such as the theorbo and the *chitarrone* [122b] with additional unstopped bass strings. Secular monodies, of which more than two hundred books were printed in Italy in the first thirty years of the century, were sung to a variety of continuo instruments, including harpsichord, clavichord, theorbo, *chitarrone*, large harp among aristocrats and Spanish guitar in light-weight pieces[2].

Italian court and household music (*musica da camera*) in this period was written for one to four string instruments with continuo, and was largely dances and sets of dancelike movements which came to be called *sonate da camera*. Sonatas played in church (*sonate da chiesa*) were composed in a more learned and sober style. The attractions of this instrumental medium brought about a revolution in the music heard in Italian churches. *Sonate da chiesa* were played in place of plainsong, which had in any case been reformed and rationalized into a dead and boring thing. Similarly, during much of the first half of the century devout attenders at Mass at St Peter's in Rome heard the famous virtuoso Girolamo Frescobaldi play his brilliant toccatas before the service, and his canzonas (in sprightly counterpoint) and ricercars (in slow and solemn counterpoint) where plainsong was formerly sung.

The earliest instrumental concertos were made by composing a trio sonata, i.e., a sonata for two violins and continuo, in such a way that a string band of whatever number of players was available could be added to it at will. Georg Muffat, a Savoyard of British descent and French training, who heard Corelli's concertos in Rome about 1682 (they were not printed until 1712), explained in the preface to his own concertos[3], which he based on Corelli's, how this *concerto grosso* was built up:

> Should you not have a great number of string players, or wish to hear these concertos with only a few, you may form a perfect trio, which is always the chief and essential group, by choosing the three parts entitled *Violino Primo Concertino*, *Violino Secundo Concertino*, and *Basso continuo e Violoncino Concertino*, using a small French bass in preference to the double or great bass called Violone [122b]; to this you may add a harpsichord or a theorbo or other similar instrument, played from the same part as the small bass. You must take care that all play loudly at the sign T or *Tutti*, and softly and tenderly at the sign S or *Solo*, as well as observing exactly the levels of loudness and softness at the words *forte* and *piano*, or at the abbreviations *f* and *p*, which mean the same thing.

The 'small French bass' was the agile six-stringed *basse de viole* which the composer Jacques Mauduit is credited with introducing in France early in the seventeenth century[4]. Muffat goes on to say that you may next add a *Viola prima*, then a *Viola secunda*. Should more players be available, you may then

> . . . add to these five parts the three remaining ones, the *Violino Primo Concerto grosso*, *Violino Secundo Concerto grosso*, and *Violone* or *Cembalo Concerto grosso* if a greater number of musicians allows of this, having each part played by a single violin, or for a fuller volume of sound by two or three together, as the number of your people and your sense suggest. In this case in order to bring out the bass of the large group

with more sonority [*majesté*] you may certainly use the double bass, which the Italians call contrabass or *Violone*. . . .

Should you have among your musicians judicious players of the *hautbois* [*des hautzbois délicats* – his German text has 'the French hautbois or shawm'] you may with success have the three parts of your trio, or *concertino*, played by two trebles and a bassoon in many of these concertos, or at least in some of their movements chosen with this in mind, taking care to choose those in keys, or to transpose them into keys, suitable to those instruments, and to put an octave higher or otherwise modify short passages which are out of their range . . .

What was the 'French oboe or shawm' to which Muffat refers? He was acquainted with French music, having been in Paris for six years in the sixteen-seventies and studied Lully's ballet style, which he had introduced to Germany in an earlier volume of his compositions[5]. The Italian-born Lully had begun his professional career as a player in the *Vingt-quatre violons du roi*, the French King's famous band of violin-family instruments. Founded by Louis XIII in 1626, this *grande bande* had been developed from the group formed in the sixteenth century by Baldassaro da Belgioioso, an Italian player who changed his name to Beaujoyeulx, for the ballets at the court of Catherine de' Medici, Queen of Henry II and until 1581 regent for her son Charles IX. Lully became the leader of the *grande bande* in 1652 and later founded *Les petits violons*, a group of twelve players with whom he aimed at the greatest perfection of small-ensemble playing. In neither group was a continuo used.

The woodwind instruments played in the French court circle were the robust shawms, used for outdoor ceremonial music, the recorder and the *musette* [123c, 124], a small finely crafted and delicately toned chamber bagpipe. Jean Hotteterre, a bagpipe maker and therefore accustomed to crafting fine reed instruments, as well as a player of the *musette* in court ballets, was the initiator of a series of experiments which led to basic changes in certain woodwind instruments. He first did a complete redesign of the recorder, making it in sections ('joints') [127, 157f]. It was this baroque recorder, not the medieval or renaissance type, which was chosen for revival in modern times. Chromatic notes (corresponding generally to the short keys on a keyboard instrument) had always been played on a finger-hole wind instrument by 'cross-fingering', i.e., putting down fingers in an order other than the direct scale-wise sequence. Constructing an instrument in joints made possible the exact boring of each part of the tube, and this in turn enabled the player to get good intonation on cross-fingered notes. It is in the nature of the recorder that cross-fingering gives good results, and this was particularly true of Hotteterre's new instrument.

With his colleagues, including Michel Philidor, Hotteterre next set about redesigning the shawm, and produced in the event a virtually new instrument, the three-jointed oboe [129, 130, 157c], known for a time outside the country of its birth as the French oboe – in England the French 'hoboy'. It had a narrow bore, small finger-holes and a completely lip-controlled reed; its cross-fingerings gave good results. The new instrument probably made its world début in Lully's ballet *L'Amour malade* in 1657, played by Hotteterre and Philidor. Its first mention in a Lully score is in the ballet *Les plaisirs de L'Isle Enchantée* of 1664, which has a '*Marche de Hautbois pour le Dieu Pan et sa Suite*'[6]. In the operas which he composed from 1673 onwards Lully used the trio of two oboes and bassoon, perhaps for the first time in *Alceste* (1674). The musical attributes which made the new instrument acceptable in this distinguished company were a dynamic range and expressive resources fully comparable with those of the violin. It seems likely that it was the manifest success of the new design which led to the forming of the *Douze hautbois du roi* [131], and that the immediate model for this group was Lully's *Petits violons*.

Jean Hotteterre and his circle were an almost uniquely ideal combination of players and craftsmen. The sweeping effect of the series of redesignings which they began were described in a letter written many years after the event (in 1740) by Michel de la Barre, a noted flautist who was in the royal corps of musicians early in the eighteenth century:

> His [i.e., Lully's] elevation meant the downfall [*chute*] of all the old instruments except the oboe, thanks to Philidor and Hotteterre, who spoiled great quantities of wood and played great quantities of music until finally they succeeded in making the instrument fit for concert use. From then on musettes were left to shepherds, and violins, recorders, theorbes and viols took their place, for the transverse flute did not arrive until later[7].

Though the depth of de la Barre's historical knowledge was not quite up to putting all the instruments in their place in the story, his picture is substantially true. As he and everybody musical in France knew, the Hotteterre dynasty had been the foremost wind instrument designers and makers in the country. In all likelihood it was they who made the new four-jointed bassoon [131, 157e], known to the English in Purcell's time as the 'French *basson*', and also the design of the new conical flute [128, 157d], with a contracting bore and three-jointed construction like the new recorder. Cross-fingered notes on the flute were less good than on the other woodwinds, and the new design was less satisfactory in the long run than the others. However, the new flute was expressive enough to have captured the amateur market from the dynamically restricted recorder by the mid-eighteenth century.

Apart from the royal bands of *violons*, string music in France in the seventeenth century was as old-fashioned as it was in England, where Purcell wrote viol consort music even in 1680. At house concerts in France only the viols were used as a family in instrumental music, commonly with *clavecin* (harpsichord) or chamber organ[8], as in England. In the second half of the century the bass viol was played as a high-grade solo instrument, notably by Marin Marais, who played and wrote for a seven-stringed instrument. The violin, flute and oboe came into use by amateurs only towards the end of the century, and here again the parallel holds with England, where tutors for these instruments began to be printed about that time. In England the technique of virtuosic variations and passage-work ('divisions') on a small bass viol, as taught in Christopher Simpson's *The Division Violist* (1659), anticipated the French development. Intermediate between the small bass and the tenor viol came the lyra viol [110], an English speciality which was said by John Playford in his *Musick's Recreation on the Lyra Viol* (1652) to have been written for first by three Jacobean composers – Daniel Farrant, Alfonso Ferrabosco II and Giovanni Coprario, the Italianized John Cooper. Playford also says that Farrant invented a lyra viol with wire sympathetic strings under the playing strings. The historical connection, if any, between this form of lyra viol and the later viola d'amore [146c] and baryton [150] is unclear.

At least from the time of Praetorius, that prolific composer and writer who kept Lutherans *au fait* with the new Italian manners, instruments and the continuo were increasingly used in Lutheran churches. The man mainly responsible for importing Italian ideas, however, was Schütz, who composed his *Psalmen* of 1619 for large vocal-instrumental ensembles of the Gabrieli kind and his first set of *Symphoniae Sacrae* of 1629, following his second stay in Venice, for small vocal-instrumental forces. The instruments he specifies are cornett, violin, recorder, flute, trumpet, trombone and *fagott*, the last a bassoon predecessor – the name was also applied later to the real bassoon. In the foreword to the second book of the *Symphoniae* (1647) (the long interval between the two books was due to the Thirty Years War) Schütz requested violinists to use a long bow-stroke so as to produce a true singing tone (*bel canto*), not the short bow-stroke which was customary in dance music. The admission of town violinists (*Stadtgeiger*) to music in church had taken place earlier in the century – in Leipzig as early as 1607 – though the town wind-players (*Stadtpfeifer*) kept their monopoly of the best weddings and the official lodgings. The main official duties of the wind-players were to sound trumpet fanfares at ten and six daily from the balcony of the tower of the Town Hall, and to play chorales on cornetts and trombones from the church towers on festivals and important civic occasions[9]. More sophisticated music to be played instead of the daily fanfares was published by the Leipzig town-musician Johann Pezel in the form of suites and sonatas[10].

In Spain, the equivalent stipendiary positions for instrumentalists were in the Church, which retained numbers of players on more or less exclusive contracts. The boys of the famous Escolania of Montserrat were trained equally in singing and in playing instruments. A special feature of Spanish baroque practice was the widespread use of the harp as a continuo instrument, alone or with an organ.

The oldest dated instrument in the Boston Museum of Fine Arts, formerly in the Galpin Collection, is a herald's trumpet with the engraved legend: '*Macht Sebastian Hainlein MCDLX*'[11]. Its maker was the first of a family engaged until about 1700 in the flourishing Nuremberg craft of brass-instrument making. Courts, cities and churches bought brass instruments from Nuremberg. The Bavarian court bought twenty trumpets, and the Brandenburg court thirty-six silver trumpets, from Isaac Ehe (*d* 1632); in 1604 Hans Schnitzer delivered to the King of Poland twenty-four silver-gilt trumpets; in 1607 Leipzig bought three trombones and two cornetts in Nuremberg; in 1669 the city itself paid Paul Hainlein, organist at St Sebald's church, for a trombone for the Frauenkirche. There were five Ehe generations continuously in business from 1612 to 1794; an Ehe daughter married J. C. Denner, wind instrument maker and generally acknowledged inventor of the clarinet[12].

The clarinet has a cylindrical tube. Even in its earliest form [142, 143, 146a] it was sounded by a separate tied-on single reed and had two keys. The keys enabled a second series of notes (an octave and a fifth, not the usual octave, above the first) to be blown, and also bridged the gap between the highest note of the first scale and the lowest note of the overblown scale. Cylindrical pipes with primitive single reeds were certainly as common on eastern European bagpipes in the seventeenth century as they are now, and at least one type of Bohemian bagpipe has a separate tied-on chanter reed. While it is impossible to say whether this antedated Denner's clarinet, it is not unlikely that the idea of experimenting with cylindrical reed pipes was suggested by some eastern European folk instrument, either bagpipe or now extinct mouth-blown pipe. Certainly the chalumeau [142a] which Denner is said to have 'improved'[13] is in its unkeyed form [157f] only a turned wooden instrument with the same acoustic behaviour as the primitive cylindrical reed pipe [17], but with a separate reed tied to a mouthpiece. Denner cannot have foreseen that this 'new sort of wind instrument, the so-called *Clarinette*' which he invented 'to the great satisfaction of music-lovers'[14] would become the most fluent and useful of all woodwind instruments [157f]. Virtuosity on the new instrument seems to have developed first in Bohemia. The famous clarinettists of the Mannheim band – for whom the earliest concertos, by the German Molter and the Bohemian Pokorny, were written – all came from Bohemia. The earliest non-Bohemian style of clarinet playing seems to have been boisterous and trumpet-like, though descriptions of the clarinet as a 'mock trumpet' may reflect the gentle sound of contemporary indoor trumpet playing rather than a brazen style on the clarinet. In the few Western scores earlier than 1750 in which clarinets appear they play simple small-compass parts, generally in pairs with one or two horns[15].

The pianoforte, the other invention of this period, made a much smaller impression on professional music-making than did the clarinet. Its prototype, and perhaps its immediate inspiration, was the large dulcimer, though a hammer action controlled from a keyboard could not yet hope to rival that instrument's *brio* when displayed by a virtuoso like Pantaleon Hebenstreit (*d* 1750). Beginning in 1709 Bartolommeo Cristofori of Florence devised a *gravicembalo col pian' e forte* (meaning a harpsichord with dynamic range by touch). This had a 'single' action, as it was later called; by 1720, the date of a surviving example [136], he was using a 'double' action, which works through a second intermediate lever and has an escapement device. The German organ and harpsichord maker Silbermann made double-action pianofortes, three of which were bought by Frederick the Great and still exist. J. S. Bach tried them and found them mildly interesting when he visited his successful son Carl Philip Emmanuel, who was Frederick's keyboardist, at Potsdam. In 1742 Johann Zumpe, a workman at Silbermann's, went to England where later he was a pioneer maker of the new instrument. Though Domenico Scarlatti's patroness and pupil Queen Maria Barbara of Spain acquired five Florentine pianos (two of which had been converted into harpsichords by 1756!) only a small handful of Scarlatti's sonatas seem to suggest by their style that he had the pianoforte in mind when writing them. The only printed music avowedly for the piano before 1750 is a set of sonatas by Ludovico Giustini of Pistoia, printed in 1732 and dedicated to Don Antonio of Portugal, Maria Barbara's uncle, and like her a pupil of Scarlatti. It was João V, Maria Barbara's father, who had captured Scarlatti, then *maestro di cappella* at St Peter's, Rome, for his chapel in Lisbon[16].

To summarize a period in which originated some of the most characteristic features of modern European instruments: the success of the makers and players of violin-family instruments took them to the leading place as ensemble instruments, rapidly in Italy, more gradually elsewhere. The German brass-instrument industry flourished greatly on a basis of established social usages at home, while France created for high artistic purposes a lead in double-reed instrument design and making which she still maintains. The functions of the church organ in Protestant Germany and Catholic France – functions generally analogous to those of instrumental *musica da chiesa* in Italy – called forth the cumulative repertory of Lutheran organ music from Samuel Scheidt to Johann Sebastian Bach, and the even production of French organists from Titelouze to Daquin. French composers, notably the Couperins, were the first to develop and exploit fully an idiomatic style of secular music for harpsichord. J. S. Bach's harpsichord music is a kaleidoscopic amalgam of German, French and Italian characteristics. Domenico Scarlatti is the supreme exponent of the imaginative and descriptive range of the harpsichord, with vivid impressions of other instruments: organ, Spanish guitar (with intriguingly dissonant chord-strumming), castanets, trumpets, horns, drums, bugles, woodwind, bagpipe and mandolin. Though the most elaborate of Maria Barbara's harpsichords had five registers, apparently including a sixteen-foot[17], the *tutti-concertino* kind of contrast on which the concerto was based is so built-in to Scarlatti's keyboard texture that it is almost gilding the lily to play him with such effusive resources. The concertos of Corelli in Rome and Torelli in Bologna, both violinists, were entirely in string monochrome. In Venice the church use of instruments which had been such a feature of the music at St Mark's in Gabrieli's and Monteverdi's times was taken over by the *ospedali* for orphans and foundlings, which became famous all over Europe for the brilliance of their chapel music. Burney's belief that it would 'receive great applause in the first opera in Europe' clearly indicates its style. Staffs of teachers trained the musical pupils of the *ospedali* to very high professional standards of skill on a variety of instruments[18]. Antonio Vivaldi, who was *maestro di violino* at the *Conservatorio dell'Ospedale della Pietà* from before 1710 and *maestro de concerti* from 1723, wrote solo parts in concertos for violin, viola, *viola d'amore,* cello, flute, recorder, oboe, clarinet, *salmo* (perhaps a large chalumeau), bassoon, trumpet, horn, lute, theorbo and mandolin[19]. The players whom J. S. Bach enlisted from among town musicians, university students and pupils at St Thomas's School for his Sunday and festival cantatas could provide a wide range of instrumental tone-colour, though very likely with less consistent virtuosity than Vivaldi's girls. Compared to Vivaldi's list, Bach's has a *violino piccolo* (a minor third higher than the violin), *violoncello piccolo* (with an additional fifth string sounding e′), *viola da gamba, oboe d'amore* (built a minor third lower than the oboe) [129], *oboe da caccia* (probably the curved *cor anglais*) timpani (only with trumpets), cornett and trombone (only to support voices), but not *salmo,* theorbo or mandolin[20]. For the visit to Venice in 1740 of Friedrich Christian, Prince of Poland and Elector of Saxony, the girls of the Pietà played three concertos preceding and between the acts of a dramatic cantata, *The Choir of the Muses.* The solo players in the first were two recorders, two theorboes, two mandolins, two *salmoe* and a cello; in the second they were *viola d'amore* and lute, with muted string accompaniment; in the third they were two violins in echo. Vivaldi was rewarded by the Conservatorio with fifteen ducats and thirteen lire for composing these three concertos and a symphony for the occasion[21]. With Bach the mark of high festivity was the splendour of trumpets and drums, which are seldom absent from cantatas for the great festivals or those for secular celebrations.

1 Printed in *Denkmäler der Tonkunst in Österreich*, x, 1903.

2 N.Fortune, 'Continuo Instruments in Italian Monodies', *Galpin Society Journal*, vi, 1953, p. 10.

3 *Ausserlesener mit Ernst- und Lust-gemengter Instrumental-Music*, 1701, reprinted in *Denkmäler der Tonkunst in Österreich*, xi (2), 1904.

4 A.Cohen, 'A Study of Instrumental Ensemble Practice in Seventeenth-Century France', *Galpin Society Journal*, xv, 1962, p. 6.

5 *Florilegia*, i and ii, 1695, 1698; reprinted in DTÖ, i (2), 1894, and ii (2), 1895.

6 J.Marx, 'The Tone of the Baroque Oboe', *Galpin Society Journal*, iv, 1951, p. 14.

7 Quoted in the original French by Marx, p. 12.

8 Cohen, p. 9.

9 C.S.Terry, *Bach's Orchestra*, 1958, pp. 15–16.

10 *Hora Decima Musicorum Lipsiensum, oder Musicalische Arbeit zum Ab-blasen um 10 Uhr Vormittag in Leipzig, bestehend in 40 Sonaten mit 5 Stimmen als 2 Cornetten und 3 Trombonen* (1670); *Musica Vespertina Lipsica, oder Leipzigische Abend-Music, bestehend in Sonaten, Praeludien, Allemanden, Couranten, Balleten, Sarabanden, Allebreven, Intraden, Capriccien . . . etc, nach der neusten heut-tagigen Manier mit 1, 2, 3, 4 oder 5 Stimmen zu spielen* (1669); specimens reprinted in *Denkmäler deutscher Tonkunst*, lxiii, 1928.

11 N.Bessaraboff, *Ancient European Musical Instruments*, 1941, p. 188.

12 W.Wörthmüller, *Die Nürnberger Trompeten- und Posaunenmacher des 17. und 18. Jahrhunderts*, 1954, passim.

13 J.G.Doppelmayr, *Historische Nachricht der Nürnbergischen Mathematicis und Künstlern*, 1730, p. 305.

14 Ibid.

15 See A.Baines, *Woodwind Instruments and their History*, 1962, pp. 298–9.

16 R.Kirkpatrick, *Domenico Scarlatti*, 1953, pp. 177–85.

17 Kirkpatrick, pp. 178, 195–206.

18 D.Arnold, 'Orphans and Ladies: the Venetian Conservatories (1680–1790)', *Proceedings of the Royal Musical Association*, 89, 1963, p. 31.

19 M.Pincherle, *Antonio Vivaldi et la musique instrumentale*, 2 vols., 1948, passim.

20 Terry, pp. 187–227.

21 Pincherle, i, p. 26.

7 *Popular patronage and changing taste 1750–1820*

Of the two newest instruments, the pianoforte seems to have appealed for some time particularly to amateurs. C. P. E. Bach, in his *Essay on the True Art of Playing Keyboard Instruments*[1], had remarkably little to say about the respective uses and merits of harpsichord, clavichord and piano. He conceded that the 'fortepiano has many advantages provided it is sturdily and well built'; he owned and played one, doing his best, he says, to compensate in his playing for its lack of sustaining power. For Dr Burney in 1772 on the Doctor's German journey C. P. E. Bach played the clavichord[2], certainly the preferred instrument in Germany, where large clavichords were built as late as 1800. C. P. E. Bach wrote his late sonatas in terms of the piano; in the last year of his life (1788) he composed a captivatingly witty concerto for harpsichord and piano, apparently the only eighteenth-century work which includes both instruments. There are several examples of instruments in which harpsichord and piano are combined [163], including two by J. A. Stein of Augsburg which have the two instruments end to end in the same case. One of these *vis-à-vis* instruments has three keyboards at the harpsichord end, from the lowest of which the piano can be played and also coupled to the harpsichord[3].

Though Farinelli, most famous of all *castrato* singers and Scarlatti's colleague at the Spanish court, inherited Maria Barbara's three best harpsichords, he told Dr Burney in his retirement that his favourite keyboard instrument was a Florentine piano of 1730 made by Cristofori's pupil Ferrini[4]. By all indications the piano was a singer's and amateur's instrument until the seventeen-sixties. Only in the seventeen-seventies did it begin to surpass the other keyboards in the estimation of professionals. One of the earliest to declare a preference was Johann Christian Bach, youngest son of J. S. and known as the 'English Bach', whose sonatas Opus V, published in London in 1765, were '*pour le clavecin ou le Piano Forte*', and all of whose later keyboard works name both instruments. J. C. Bach played a solo on the pianoforte in 1768 at a benefit concert for J. C. Fischer, the famous oboist who had just arrived from Germany, and who later married Mary Gainsborough. Bach probably played a sonata from his Opus V; he certainly played on a Zumpe square [162], for he gave Zumpe a cheque for fifty pounds in the same month as the concert[5].

J. C. Bach created a style of piano music which appealed to English audiences, but was not so difficult as to discourage the competent amateur. Mozart visited London in 1764 at the age of eight, and in the following year took without acknowledgement – a common practice at the time – three sonatas from J. C. Bach's Opus V and turned them into piano concertos for his own concerts. Twelve years later Mozart visited Stein's workshop, where he tried a piano about which he felt a professional could be really enthusiastic [164]. The action designed by Stein came to be known as the Viennese action, and was used by many other makers. The Viennese piano with its leather-covered hammers and extremely light touch is the ideal medium for Mozart's piano music. Specimens are extremely rare, but modern essays in the re-creation of the type [246] give some idea of its bright but delicate sound. In 1818 Broadwood presented Beethoven with a piano of the larger and heavier type [183] with which the English maker had been experimenting for some ten years; it had a compass of six octaves, as against the earlier five to five and a half. This kind of piano, not the lighter Viennese type, was the basis of the later development of the instrument.

The repute of London piano makers, immigrant and native, is shown by a list of musical instruments confiscated from nobles and wealthy bourgeois at the French Revolution. Thirty of the sixty-four pianos were by English makers: Zumpe, his successor Schoene, Berger (properly Beyer), Beck, Pohlmann and Qanter. Of the sixty-two harpsichords listed only one was English – a new Broadwood[6]. The rate of change-over from harpsichord to piano making may be illustrated by the case of Dublin, a busy capital city before the union with England in 1800. In a list of Irish instrument makers[7] the first year in which a piano maker is shown is 1786; in 1790 there were two makers of harpsichords only and three of both harpsichords and pianos, while in 1795 there were five makers of pianos only and four of both instruments. The advantages of the piano for amateur use were clearly proclaimed by dealers in the United States; one of the first pianofortes to be imported there was ordered in 1771 by Thomas Jefferson as a present for his fiancée Mrs Skelton. The making of pianos began in America about 1775. They sold well, and some of the reasons are given in a New York advertisement of 1792:

The forte-piano is become so exceedingly fashionable in Europe that few polite families are without it. This much-esteemed instrument forms an agreeable accompaniment for the female voice, takes up but little room, may be moved with ease, and consequently kept in tune with little attention – so that it is on that account superior to the harpsichord. The improvements which Messrs Dodds & Claus have made in the Forte-Piano have rendered it much more acceptable than those imported. The introduction of their new invented hammers and dampers is acknowledged to be a great improvement, as also the means they have taken to prepare their wood to stand the effects of our climate, which imported instruments never do, but are sure to suffer not only from the agitation of the vessel, but from the saline qualities of the seas[8].

Unlike the pianoforte, the clarinet in the first phase of its history was an instrument of professional virtuosi, who exploited to the full its wide compass and dynamic range, its great mobility and the dramatic contrast between the parts of its compass. By 1775 clarinet-players were available in Milan, Lyons, Paris, London and Oxford, though apparently not in Vienna, Dresden, Leipzig or Berlin[9]. The presence or absence of a permanent opera, and if present its degree of progressiveness, probably had something to do with this distribution. Between 1770 and 1784 twelve concertos in the most graceful rococo style were composed by Carl Stamitz, son of the Johann who had made the Mannheim orchestra famous. Most of them were for the Bohemian composer-virtuoso Joseph Beer, who was for some time clarinettist to the Duke of Orleans in Paris. The clarinet's musical personality was clearly delineated by the time Mozart composed his delicious trio for clarinet, viola and piano in 1786, the clarinet quintet in 1787, and the concerto in 1791, all with Anton Stadler in mind as soloist. Like all eighteenth-century writers for the clarinet, Mozart avoided its extreme high register and was careful about the few touchy places the instrument still had. From the late eighteenth century until about 1840, a period during which the mechanism of the clarinet was being steadily advanced, virtuosi like H. J. Baermann displayed its varied qualities in travels which anticipated in their scope the recital tours of Paganini and Liszt. It was for Baermann that Weber wrote his two concertos and other virtuoso pieces, and Mendelssohn his two trios for clarinet, basset-horn and piano.

Clarinet playing by amateurs, which was probably rare until after the seventeen-forties [146a], was general enough in England [173] by about 1780 to justify the printing of the first known tutor for the instrument, entitled *The Clarinet Instructor . . . by a capital performer . . . to which is added several Duo's . . . and a Quintetto for Horns, Clarinets and a Bassoon.* The French tutors by A. Vanderhagen (1785) and M. F. Blasius (c 1795) were clearly for professional training, while the *Méthode de clarinette . . . adoptée par le Conservatoire* (1802) by J. X. Lefèvre, first professor of the instrument at the Paris Conservatoire, was for the new plan of professional musical education set up in republican France.

A century earlier a completely double-reed band had been used for marching music such as Lully wrote for the foot-soldiers of Louis XIV. In 1762 the Swiss Guard of Louis XV was permitted to form a band of four clarinets, four oboes, four horns and four bassoons[10]; this use of mixed instrumentation has been characteristic of large army bands ever since. The number of ensemble groups with clarinets must have been increasing rapidly in France, for a work on composing for them was printed in 1764; this was Valentin Roeser's brief *Essai d'instruction à l'usage de ceux qui composent pour la clarinette et le cor avec des remarques sur l'harmonie et des exemples à deux clarinettes, deux cors et deux bassons.* One of his examples was a piece for two clarinets and two horns by Johann Stamitz, who, Roeser said, had 'the best knowledge of the true nature of wind instruments'[11]. *Harmonie* is the French term for an ensemble of brass and woodwinds, military or civil; in England the term 'military band' is used with the same meaning. The real history of organized army bands began in post-revolutionary France. Meanwhile the single-reed family of instruments had been enlarged by the development about 1770 by Anton and Michel Mayrhofer of Passau in Bavaria of the basset-horn [177], which quickly came into use in Germany, Austria, Hungary and Bohemia. However, virtually no notice of it was taken at this time in France. Mozart included it in serenades and other wind music after his move from Salzburg to Vienna in 1781.

The first military band of the French Republic was planned in 1795 at the newly founded Paris Conservatoire, where François Joseph Gossec, who had been notably enterprising in the instrumentation of some of his compositions, had an important influence. The band consisted of a flute, six clarinets, three bassoons, a trumpet, two horns, a serpent [157a, 172, 173], bass drum [175] and cymbals. Except in Prussia, army music in this sense did not come into existence in Germany until much later. In the England of the early nineteenth century the size and composition of a regimental band seem still to have been largely left to the individual commanding officer. In 1823 official sanction was given for fourteen players and a bandmaster. The band of the United States Marines in 1817 had fourteen members: two flutes, five clarinets, two horns, a bugle, a trumpet, a trombone, a bassoon and a drummer. In 1821 it had twenty members[12].

For professional music for small ensembles the string quartet and quintet were much favoured in German and Austrian courts and houses of aristocratic patrons, though they were hardly known elsewhere. The larger ensembles which played symphonies and accompanied solo concertos (relatively few concertos were written for more than one solo instrument) had varying complements of woodwind and brass, from which two oboes and two horns were seldom omitted. A run-through of Haydn symphonies available in print shows that oboes are absent from four symphonies up to No. 40 (one of the four has *cor anglais*) and horns from two others. Flute, bassoon, trumpet and timpani are very rare up to No. 60 (1775). The Paris symphonies (Nos. 82–7), composed on commission for the *Concerts de la Loge Olympique* in 1785–6, all have two flutes, two oboes, two bassoons and two horns, and two of them have two trumpets and two timpani in addition. The last thirteen (92–104; 1788–95), comprising the 'Oxford' to acknowledge his honorary degree and those composed for the two series of concerts organized by Salomon in London, all have trumpets and timpani, and five of the second set have clarinets as well. In the minuet of his first symphony (1800) Beethoven treated the woodwind section as a complete unit, leading the Viennese critics to complain that he made the orchestra sound like a wind band. For reinforced instrumentation in the symphonies Beethoven added at various times a third horn, a fourth horn, three trombones, piccolo and contrabassoon.

Though in some German and Austrian courts instrumental ensembles shared players with the orchestra of the opera [153], the composition of the opera orchestra was governed by its functional history and by the associative use of instruments. For example, hunting horns of the close-coiled helical form were sounded for hunting scenes in an opera by Cavalli in 1639 and in a ballet by Lully in 1664. The former was a fanfare, in five parts, of the kind Purcell imitated with strings in the hero's hunt in *Dido and Aeneas*; the latter was a more complex fanfare effect, also for five horns[13]. With the increasing adoption from about 1650 onwards of a hoop-like form with two or three coils [135, 146b], there seems to have been a bifurcation of functions, whereby the technique of using the higher harmonics on the upper horn or pair of horns in a small horn group was exploited equally by players at hunting ceremonials and public festivities, particularly in France and England, and by players of indoor ensemble music, particularly in Bohemia, Germany and Italy. Handel included horns in his *Water Music* (c 1715), where they were used for the first time in a mixed instrumental group in England, as part of a festive outdoor entertainment. Noble hosts were accustomed to have horn playing in the open air for their guests; when Queen Caroline visited the Duke of Newcastle at Claremont in 1729 they 'walked till candle-light, being entertained with very fine French horns'. In 1717 Lady Mary Wortley Montague wrote from Paris about a ball during the carnival festivities: 'the music good, if they had not that detestable custom of mixing hunting horns with it, that almost deafen the company'.

In ensemble music the French horn had already been exploited in Bohemia and Saxony before it was heard in Paris – for example, in 1751 in a symphony by Johann Stamitz. In 1754 the orchestra of the patron La Pouplinière, then directed by Stamitz, had both horns and clarinets[14]. In 1763, when Gossec was director, this orchestra consisted of a solo violin, two first violins, two second violins, a flute, an oboe, two clarinets who also played horns, a bassoon, two harps, one of whom also played a horn, a cello, a double bass and a harpsichord[15].

Horn and trumpet parts in early symphonies are simple and restrained, having little or no trace of the virtuoso techniques of the late Baroque era. It is likely that social changes in Germany meant the end of the town musicians as they had formerly existed, and therefore the end of *clarin* trumpet playing. Virtuosity on the horn, however, went on right through the century, and was facilitated by the technique of 'stopping' by putting a hand in the bell, which added many semitones to the scale of the instrument, and also enabled the player to correct the intonation of flat or sharp harmonics. The elementary nature of symphonic horn parts suggests that the ability of the average player was much below that of such virtuosi as Rodolphe, who introduced hand-stopping in the Paris Opera in 1765, or the famed Punto, who impressed London with it in 1770 or 1771[16]. More probably, displays of virtuosity on any single instrument would have been out of keeping with the musical and social functions of the symphony, which in the eighteenth century was essentially medium-scale music for a mixed ensemble with the emphasis very much on the strings, not the large-scale dramatic form it later became. In England, the musical elephantiasis of the Handel Commemoration in Westminster Abbey in 1784 [174], and of similar monstrosities since that time, could doubtless be partly accounted for by the habit of church and civil authorities – known nowadays as the 'Establishment' – of falling back on the proclamation of religious and moral tenets in the face of social problems.

Though Praetorius had made a small bow towards European folk instruments and non-European instruments, the first writer to treat them from an unbiased humanistic point of view was the Jesuit priest Filippo Bonanni in his *Gabinetto Armonico*, with engravings by Arnold van Westerhout, which was first printed in Rome in 1716, was reprinted with additions in 1722 and appeared in a French edition in 1776[17]. In 1770 Père Amiot, a Jesuit missionary, published the first useful account of Chinese instruments. His importation into Europe of the *sheng*, the Chinese free-reed mouth organ, aroused an interest in free reeds [201] which aided the invention, later, of the mouth-blown harmonica and the bellows-blown concertina [203] and harmonium[18]. Certain Turkish instruments came into European instrumentation after 1750. They were used for playing pseudo-Turkish music, as in Mozart's *The Abduction from the Seraglio*, and for playing Western march-music, as in Haydn's 'Military' symphony (No. 100, 1794) and in the 'heroic action' verse of the Ode to Joy in Beethoven's Ninth symphony (1823). Each composer used bass drum (which should be played with stick and switch [175b], but seldom is), cymbals and triangle, the characteristic percussion of the bands of Janissaries, who were the infantry of the Ottoman Turks. At this time a full Janissary band might comprise nine *zurna* (shawms), nine *chaghana*, called 'Jingling Johnny' or 'Turkish Crescent' in the West, nine bass drums, nine cymbals, nine *naqqāra* (small kettle-drums) and nine *buru* (trumpets), a total of fifty-four members. The composer and poet C. F. D. Schubart described the Janissary music in terms which remind us of the impact of Saracen music on the Crusaders:

> The character of this music is so warlike that even cowardly souls take courage. Anyone who has had the good fortune to hear the real Janissaries, whose ensemble is commonly eighty to a hundred strong, must really laugh at the poor imitations which go with us by the name of Turkish music. At a concert of Turkish music given to honour Achmet Effendi, the Turkish ambassador in Berlin, he shook his head indignantly and said: 'It is not Turkish!' Since then, however, the King of Prussia has taken actual Turks into his service and introduced the true Turkish music into some of his regiments. In Vienna too the Emperor maintains an excellent ensemble of Turkish musicians, whom the great Gluck has already used in his operas. . . . No other genre of music requires so firm, decided and overpoweringly predominant a beat. The first beat of each bar is so strongly marked with a new and manly accent that it is virtually impossible to get out of step[19].

With these qualities it is not surprising that Janissary percussion was adopted in military bands, and later in a modified form in the orchestra.

By far the most widely dispersed musical *exotica* in the late eighteenth and early nineteenth centuries were the Highland Scottish dance tunes and the non-Italian-school style of playing them on the fiddle. These were exported from their native regions partly as a result of the deliberate clearances of population from the Highlands from 1780 to 1854. Even before 1780 Highland fiddling had spread through the Lowlands of Scotland and to England; from the last quarter of the century onwards the fiddle tunes of players like William Marshall and Neil Gow were widely sought after, and were given to the public in such collections as Neil Gow's six issues of strathspeys and reels, printed at Dunkeld from 1784 to 1822. The rhythmic idioms of the dances caught on all over western Europe, and Beethoven, Weber, Schubert, Chopin and many others catered to the fashion with pseudo-Scottish pieces called *Écossaises*. The eighteenth-century idea that no civilized music could exist without a bass, as well as the use of the piano as a maid-of-all-work which we take for granted, are implicit in the commissioning by the Edinburgh publisher George Thomson of Pleyel and Kozeluch, and later Haydn and Beethoven, to provide piano accompaniments for Scottish, Irish and Welsh songs. Beethoven felt the dichotomy between the idioms of the tunes and his customary style, for he wrote to Thomson in 1818: 'One very quickly finds chords to harmonize such songs, but to succeed in matching the simplicity, the character, the nature of the song – that is not always as easy for me as you might think'[20]. Unfortunately, the way of setting tunes from a musical tradition other than their own which Beethoven and his contemporaries established prevailed in general until the beginning of the present century.

From the late seventeenth century onwards Irish music, like Highland Scottish, emerged from an archaic society into a society preoccupied with the artistic styles and manners proper to 'rational' people. In the course of the eighteenth century the traditional craft of the Irish professional harpers, wrenched from its context of panegyrics and heroic tales, finally spent itself in vain attempts on the part of O'Carolan and others to adapt its musical speech to eighteenth-century taste – an opposite fate to that which befell Scottish dance music. The enthusiastic amateur Edward Bunting salvaged some of the ruins at a harpers' competition festival which he organized in Belfast in 1792, but it took the ministrations of Tom Moore as poet and tune-doctor, and Sir John Stevenson as provider of piano parts, to make the Irish tunes acceptable to a European audience. With newly styled accompaniments by a series of composers including Balfe and Britten, Moore's *Irish Melodies* has been a steady seller all over Europe. The considerable variety of harps which had existed in the Baroque era[21] was reduced during the latter part of the eighteenth century by the widespread acceptance of the single-action pedal harp, an instrument of greater chromatic flexibility though probably less interesting tone quality. A method of changing temporarily the pitch of the strings by means of mechanism operated from pedals [157b] was first patented by the Bavarian maker Hochbrucker in 1720, and the final form of mechanization – a double action with two modifications of string length from each pedal – was patented in 1810 by Sebastian Érard of London. The application to the harp of chromatic mechanism seems to have entailed a considerable curtailment of its musical effectiveness. Apart from Berlioz's beautiful writing for the instrument, and some display music of transient appeal, the real repertoire of the pedal harp, both solo and orchestral, consists largely of music composed in the twentieth century.

1 English edition by W.J.Mitchell, 1949.

2 P.A.Scholes, *The Great Dr Burney*, i, 1948, p. 238.

3 R.Russell, *The Harpsichord and Clavichord*, 1959, p. 109, pl. 95.

4 R.Kirkpatrick, *Domenico Scarlatti*, 1953, pp. 175–6.

5 C.S.Terry, *John Christian Bach*, 1929, p. 112.

6 A.G.Hess, 'The Transition from Harpsichord to Piano', *Galpin Society Journal*, vi, 1953, pp. 83–90.

7 J.Teahan, 'A List of Irish Instrument Makers', *Galpin Society Journal*, xvi, 1963, p. 28.

8 R.Benton, 'The Early Piano in the United States', *Music: Libraries and Instruments*, 1961, p. 179.

9 F.G.Rendall, *The Clarinet*, 1954, p. 82.

10 Ibid., p. 79.

11 Facsimiles in *Die Musik in Geschichte und Gegenwart*, s.v. 'Instrumentation'.

12 H.G.Farmer, *Military Music*, 1950, pp. 39–44.

13 R.Morley Pegge, *The French Horn*, 1960, pp. 13, 80–4.

14 G.Gucuel, *La Pouplinière et la musique de chambre au xviiie siècle*, 1913, p. 319.

15 Ibid., pp. 336–9.

16 Morley Pegge, pp. 88, 91.

17 Ed. F.Ll.Harrison and J.Rimmer, 1964.

18 J.Howarth, 'Free-Reed Instruments', *Musical Instruments through the Ages*, ed. A.Baines, 1961, p. 321.

19 L.Schubart, ed., *C.F.D.Schubart's Ideen zu einer Ästhetik der Tonkunst*, Vienna, 1806, pp. 330–1.

20 E.Anderson, *The Letters of Beethoven*, ii, 1961, p. 756.

21 J.Rimmer, 'James Talbot's Manuscript: VI. Harps', *Galpin Society Journal*, xvi, 1963, p. 63.

8 Industrialization and the great public 1820–1918

In his *Souvenirs*, written in 1886, the French writer and artist Ernest Legouvé tells of an evening at the Paris Opera in 1832 when a young man in the second gallery suddenly leaped to his feet, trembling with rage, during Caspar's song in Weber's *Der Freischütz*, and yelled at the orchestra: 'You don't want two flutes there, you brutes, you want two piccolos. Two piccolos, do you hear. Oh, the brutes!'[1] The young man was Hector Berlioz, whose own *Mémoires* cite many instances of operas being chopped about by adapters such as Castil-Blaze – 'this musical horse-doctor', as Berlioz calls him – of scores being tampered with by conductors ('does not one hear in London bass drum, trombone and ophicleide parts which Mr Costa has added to the scores of *Don Giovanni*, *Figaro* and *The Barber of Seville*?'), and of parts being modified by players[2]. Guillon, the flautist at the Opera, roused Berlioz's scorn by his habit of taking liberties with Gluck, such as playing the low notes in the sacred march in *Alceste* an octave higher, so that he was sure to be heard. Berlioz, by making an intense study of opera scores and performances, and by getting players to make experiments for him on their instruments, learnt to perceive 'the subtle link between musical communication and the particular art of instrumentation', on which he later (1844) wrote one of the earliest modern treatises. As a student he experienced little purely instrumental music, taking no pleasure in the concerts at the Opera, where symphonies by Haydn and Mozart ('which are generally of an intimate character') were played by a feeble orchestra on a large and acoustically poor stage. At the orchestral concerts of the *Société des concerts du Conservatoire*, which were founded in 1828, the Beethoven performances conducted by Habaneck caused a great sensation, though they were not always authentic in their instrumentation (as indeed happens today with music of other composers). During the following two decades it was Berlioz himself who, with a brilliance and originality it is difficult to appreciate today, showed Paris audiences many of the possibilities of the new dramatic instrumentation.

Unlike many composers Berlioz was a lively eared and articulate observer of all kinds of musical performance. His sparkling accounts of his experiences as a Prix de Rome prizewinner in Italy in 1831–2 and as a touring composer-conductor in the eighteen-forties vividly reveal the new musical structure of post-Napoleonic Europe. In Rome the band for the Papal procession on Corpus Christi was an 'impious, coarse cacophony of two groups of quacking clarinets, roaring trombones, furious bass drums and clownish trumpets'. Naples was the only Italian city where he could really say there was music worth listening to. Otherwise his musical delights were improvising scenes from the *Aeneid* to his own guitar [186], and listening to the music of peasants – which at any rate had simplicity and character, as he says. He writes about a vigorous rustic love-song, accompanied by an enormous mandolin, a bagpipe and a little triangle; about the cloaked and hatted Abruzzi musicians in Rome playing traditional Christmas music on a bag-pipe [240] backed up by a large *piffero* (shawm) doubling the bass, with the tune on a smaller shawm, and above that showers of bizarre ornamentation on two tiny shawms played by teenagers; and again about playing his guitar to the endless demands of great dark-haired peasant girls that *questa signore qui suona la chitarra francese* should improvise *saltarelli* for their dancing to the tambourine.

On Berlioz's conducting tour Fétis put at his disposal the total orchestral forces of the Brussels Conservatoire, consisting of two hundred players. The Frankfurt Opera orchestra of forty-seven players – about the usual number in smaller German towns – was first-rate, with exquisite winds and only the defect common in Germany of brassy tone in the horns, especially when forcing high notes. The Stuttgart orchestra was vigorous and fiery, and had an excellent harpist, a rarity in Germany. Unfortunately, however, the first flute played on an antiquated instrument with poor tone and defective upper register, and also had the bad habit of introducing trills and other ornaments not indicated by the composer. Berlioz remarked on the power of the trombones; the horns, too brassy as at Frankfurt, were the new rotary valve horns which Adolphe Sax had proved to be better than the piston type. The rotary valve system was coming in all over Germany for horns (Leipzig held out against them for some time yet), and for trumpets, bombardons and tubas, though the Stuttgart military band still used the inferior two-piston trumpet. Berlioz was amazed at the sight-reading ability of the Stuttgart orchestra, which read and mastered his *Symphonie fantastique* and *Francs-Juges* over-ture at sight. In the Black Forest village of Hechingen he conducted the small orchestra of the feudal Prince in several pieces of his own with modified orchestration – third and fourth horns written into the viola parts, harp part on the piano, trumpet and trombone parts stripped to a few notes.

At Mannheim there was a 'very intelligent little orchestra', but the trombones could not manage the 'Brigands' Orgy' in *Harold en Italie*, and there was no ophicleide, which was needed for all the big new orchestral works. Weimar had an 'extraordinarily powerful' rotary valve trumpet, but no *cor anglais*, no harp and no ophicleide. At Leipzig, with Mendelssohn in charge, the Subscription Concerts Society had a magnificent choir, excellent orchestra and a perfect concert hall in their Gewandhaus. Berlioz got twenty-four violins instead of the sixteen which had never before been exceeded, but no *cor anglais*, harp or ophicleide could be found – Mendelssohn played the harp solos on the piano. The orchestra played excellently, and Ferdinand David, their leader, played Berlioz's *Rêverie et Caprice* superbly. At Dresden Berlioz found a young and cooperative *Kapellmeister* named Richard Wagner, as good an orchestra and wind band as anywhere in Germany, a spirit of rivalry with Leipzig, admiration for his *Requiem*, and puzzlement at the *Symphonie fantastique*. There was a good *cor anglais*, but the first oboe had the old-fashioned mania for added ornaments, and even dared to introduce them in his solo at the beginning of the *Scène aux champs* in the *Symphonie fantastique*. The reeds of the military band were not irreproachable, and would have benefited, Berlioz thought, by having clarinets from 'the incomparable Sax'. There were no ophicleides, the low instruments being 'Russian bassoons' (a form of upright serpent), serpents and tubas. In Dresden Berlioz encountered Parish-Alvars, the famous English touring virtuoso on the double-action harp, and was rhapsodic about his fantasia on Rossini's *Moses* (which had been imitated on the piano by Thalberg) and his variations in harmonics on the 'Chorus of Mermaids' from Weber's *Oberon*. At Brunswick the harpist, with the old-fashioned single-action harp [180], practised the solo part in *Harold en Italie* assiduously, but lost his place in the concert through an attack of nerves. The ophicleide part was managed after a fashion by the Russian bassoon. Hanover was strong in solo winds, and the bassoons played in tune, unhappily a very rare thing. Darmstadt had a remarkable virtuoso on the four-stringed double bass, who displayed his instrument's capacity for sounding broad and noble adagios. The most impressive orchestra was that at Berlin under Meyerbeer, who was then director of the King of Prussia's music. It had fifty-four strings, two harps and quadruple woodwind and brass. Berlioz observed that quadruple woodwind allowed for additional pairs in the loudest passages to balance the power of the brass. Berlin was alive with military bands; the chief bandmaster W. F. Wieprecht, inventor of the tuba (with G. W. Moritz) in 1835, had about six hundred players under him, with standards of intonation and ability in playing high notes on trumpets, horns and cornets which no French band could match. The Crown Prince of Prussia ordered a private performance by three hundred and twenty players conducted by Wieprecht to be given for Berlioz's enjoyment. The programme began with the *Francs-Juges* overture in a wind-band arrangement the composer had never heard, and the clarinets distinguished themselves in a grand Battle Symphony composed for two orchestras by the English ambassador, the Earl of Westmorland, better known as Lord Burghersh.

Summarizing his impressions as a pioneer barnstorming conductor, Berlioz admitted that he had been for some time opposed to valve horns. However, actual experiments had convinced him that there was no perceptible difference in tone-quality or sonority. The fault lay with players who neglected to use hand-stopping, which was still called for in some circumstances, and with composers who failed to mark in their scores the notes which should be hand-stopped. There was even less reason, he considered, to deprecate the valve trumpet, which lost nothing in brilliance compared to the natural trumpet. Germany was superior in brass in general; French military bands had as yet neither valve trumpets – this was because of the popularity of the *cornet-à-pistons*, whose tone was less noble than the trumpet's – nor tubas. The five-valve tuba which Wieprecht introduced in Prussia, and of which Sax made admirable specimens, had marked advantages over the ophicleide [191], which judging from Berlioz's account had little vogue in Germany. In the woodwind department the German clarinettists were better than the French, the oboists about equal, and the flautists inferior, for the flute was nowhere played as it was in Paris. In respect to some instruments the Germans were markedly inferior; these were *cor anglais*, ophicleide, harp, kettle-drums (except for Wieprecht, who played them 'like a clap of thunder'), bass drum and cymbals (which were nearly always cracked or chipped, even in the best orchestras).

Berlioz's experiences took place at the time when the manufacturing processes of the Industrial Revolution were being applied to the technology of musical instruments. In this sphere the most sweeping change which these processes, and the standards of precision which went with them, brought about was the liberation of brass instruments from the limitations of the natural harmonic series by means of the piston valve [187] patented in 1818 jointly by Heinrich Stölzel, horn-player and repairer to the King of Prussia, and Friedrich Bluhmel, a mining-company bandsman in Berlin[3]. Throughout the nineteenth century experiments with the mechanisms of musical instruments were continuously on the boil, and were greatly stimulated by the holding of industrial exhibitions. Following the invention of the rotary valve [188] by Joseph Riedl of Vienna in 1832[4], improvements in the operation of both types of valve, which have exactly the same function of varying the fundamental length of tube and thus the harmonic series available to the player, continued into the present century. With the trumpet the new freedom had no attendant penalties, as Berlioz pointed out. Like Berlioz, many composers and professional players in the first half of the nineteenth century opposed the introduction of the valve horn. Even Wagner, in an introductory note to the score of

Tristan and Isolde (1865), compared its tone unfavourably with that of the hand-horn, and envisaged, like Berlioz, the use of hand-stopping on the valve horn, marking stopped notes with a plus sign, which became the normal indication:

> The composer thinks the treatment of the horns merits careful attention. Owing to the introduction of valves, the gain to this instrument has been so great that it is impossible to ignore these accessories, although the horn has thereby undoubtedly lost some of its beauty of tone and especially some of its capability of delicate slurring. On account of this great loss, the composer, with whom the true character of the horn rests, ought certainly to abstain from the use of valve-horns, had not experience on the other hand taught him that clever artists by particularly careful handling are able to reduce to a minimum the above disadvantages, so that as regards tone and slurring hardly any difference is perceptible. In anticipation of the inevitable improvement in valve-horns, horn players are strongly advised to study very carefully their several parts in the following score. . . . Single notes marked with a + signify stopped notes; and should these occur in keys in which they are open, it is always assumed that the player changes the key with the valves, so that the note is given as a stopped note[5].

Until late in the nineteenth century a programme of orchestral music without soloists was a rare event. Whether the concert was organized by a concert-giving society, or instigated by an individual instrumentalist (this kind was called in England a 'benefit' concert), the band merely punctuated with symphonies and overtures a formidably long programme of virtuosic vocal and instrumental solos, and accompanied instrumental concertos. The seventh and penultimate concert of the Philharmonic Society during the London season (February to June) of 1827, for example, included symphonies by Haydn and Beethoven (the 'Pastoral'), overtures by Cherubini and Peter von Winter (the forgotten composer of more than thirty operas), and concertos played by Liszt and Bériot. At the previous concert the instrumental soloist had been the great flautist Charles Nicholson, who played from manuscript his own 'Fantasia on *Au clair de la Lune*'. The final variation in this work was described by a reviewer of its printed form as 'most completely illustrative of Mr N.'s style, and exquisite it is when heard with the rich tone he produces on his lower notes'. 'Mr Nicholson,' the reviewer also observed, 'allowed every where in England to be *le premier de son espèce*, has been amongst the first to introduce a better and more solid style into his compositions, to address them to the understandings as well as the ears of his hearers, and thus to assert the dignity of his instrument'[6]. Examples of Nicholson's style of ornamentation in such pieces as '*Ah perdona*' from Mozart's *La Clemenza di Tito* and 'Cease your funning' from *The Beggar's Opera* are extant in tutors he published for his instrument[7]. It was Nicholson's playing of the eight-keyed flute [193*b*] which started the Munich player, craftsman and inventor Theobald Boehm on his long course of controlled experiment with, and step-by-step redesigning of, this instrument. The result was the most thorough overhaul of any woodwind design since the Hotteterres. The Boehm-system cylindrical flute, devised in 1847 [194], was produced with detail improvements by makers in France and England, and became the recognized professionals' instrument in those countries, though players in the country of its invention were slower to adopt it.

About 1811 Iwan Müller, a Russian-born touring composer-virtuoso on the clarinet, devised a clarinet with thirteen keys (seven more than the number then normal) and applied for official recognition of his instrument by the national conservatories of France. The answer to such an application was the chief factor in the fortunes of a new design in republican France. In this case it was unfavourable, the advising body (which included Gossec, Cherubini and Méhul) taking the view that if the new clarinet were exclusively adopted composers would be deprived of the different and distinctive tone qualities of the normal clarinets in C, B flat and A[8]. Elsewhere later versions of Müller's clarinet [199] had more success, and a development of this kind of clarinet is still widely used in Germany and Russia. Even before Boehm achieved the final form of his flute design, a clarinet by the Paris maker Auguste Buffet using the principles of Boehm's flute mechanism had been awarded a medal at the Paris Exhibition of 1839, and was later (1844) patented jointly by Buffet and Klosé, professor of clarinet at the Conservatoire[9]. With Klosé's backing it was officially adopted in France and later was used by French players in the United States. It was not generally used in England until after 1900 [200].

The fully keyed modern form of the oboe was created in France, as its two-keyed predecessor had been, and again through the work of player-craftsmen who were virtually assured in advance of its official adoption. Henri Brod, a Conservatoire-trained player who became second oboe at the Opera in 1810 at the age of twenty, showed at the Paris Exhibition of 1839 (the year in which he died) an oboe with improved key-work, the first straight *cor anglais* (*cor anglais moderne*) [197], and the first machine for precision gouging of the cane from which reeds are made. The brothers Charles-Louis and Frédéric Triébert, who inherited the family instrument-making firm in 1848, were likewise Conservatoire products – Charles-Louis had been the best oboe student of his year. Their gradual refinement of the design of the oboe through successive stages (called *systèmes*) [196a and b] over the forty or so years during which they held contracts to the national institutions gave French oboes a lead over those of all other countries[10]. It was a German band-master, Carl Almenraeder, who about 1825 designed for the benefit of his numerous trainee bandsmen a bassoon [202b] more reliable in operation than the normal profes-sional instrument of the time. The benefits of Almenraeder's design, however, were gained at the expense of tone quality. The modern German bassoon, which is now used in most countries except France and Belgium, was the successful outcome of steps taken by the Heckel company of Biebrich-am-Rhein to counter this loss. This they achieved by 1879, when the Heckel bassoon, which restored to the instrument something of its old singing quality, is said to have been played for the first time in the Wagner Opera-House in Bayreuth.

The importance in French musical life of official support for new ideas is again apparent in the story of 'the incomparable Sax'. In the eighteen-forties the opposition of his rivals, as Berlioz later recalled it, was such that his workmen were enticed away, his designs stolen and his resources wasted in lawsuits. It was clear to Berlioz that if the French military bands were to reach the standards set by the Prussian and Austrian bands it was essential that they should have valve trumpets and tubas. An order from the Ministry of War for three hundred trumpets and a hundred tubas, he thought, would save Sax from bankruptcy. Fortunately for Sax he had some influential friends, and his invention, the saxophone [192], was accepted by the French military authorities in 1847, the year after he patented it. Made in many sizes, it combines a single-reed mouth-piece with a wide conical bore, thus having the easy emission of the clarinet and the octave overblowing of the oboe. French and French-type military bands have used it ever since, though it has not to any extent taken root in Germany. Jean Georges Kastner, who printed a treatise on instrumentation seven years before Berlioz's more famous work, wrote a solo for the alto saxophone in his biblical opera *Le dernier roi de Juda* (1844), as did a number of other French opera composers, including Bizet and Saint-Saens. This 'classical' tradition of solo and ensemble saxophone playing, as distinct from the modern jazz tradition, is still a French speciality.

A range of valved brass instruments with bugle-like bore had been developed in Germany by 1840 (this included the Wieprecht-Moritz tuba which so impressed Berlioz).

The rather variable names for these instruments include saxhorn, flugelhorn, tenor horn, baritone, euphonium and tuba. The wider use of this kind of instrument was due to Sax, who patented his family of saxhorns [190] in 1845. Following the recommendation of an official Commission on music in the French army, saxhorns were also adopted in the military bands of the Republic[11].

Various forms of low-pitched clarinet were experimented with during the eighteenth and early nineteenth centuries. It was for an experimental instrument, possibly one devised by Buffet and the noted clarinettist J. F. Dacosta, that Meyerbeer wrote a solo in *Les Huguenots* (1836). The true bass clarinet seems virtually to have been invented by Sax, himself a capable player of the clarinet, and was his first patent (1838)[12]. Liszt and Wagner wrote for the instrument in orchestral scores in the eighteen-forties. The Royal Artillery Band, the most accomplished of the English army bands, had begun to use saxophones in 1848; by 1863 they had been replaced by bass clarinets, and the band did not use saxophones again until the twentieth century[13].

In the eighteenth century the name 'harmonica' had been used for the musical glasses, which, as perfected by Benjamin Franklin about 1761, were actually glass bowls. Gluck appeared as a player of the earlier form of the glass harmonica in London in 1746, and it was for a blind performer on the later form, Maria Kirchgessner, that Mozart wrote his *Adagio and Rondo* (K.617) for harmonica, flute, oboe, viola and cello in 1791. In the early nineteenth century the name became attached to an entirely different type of instrument. Various experiments with free reeds led in 1818 to the invention by Haeckl of Vienna of a small reed organ called *Physharmonica* (i.e., bellows harmonica), and eventually to the invention by Debain of Paris in 1848 of the harmonium, which was later given 'stops' and other refinements, notably by Alexandre and Mustel of Paris.

The mouth organ (*Mundharmonica*) was developed by C. F. L. Buschmann of Berlin in 1821–2, and by Sir Charles Wheatstone, the English physicist, inventor of a kaleidophone, and an important contributor to the development of the telegraph, with his 'symphonium' of 1829 [201]. Since 1857 the mouth organ [232a] has been the particular speciality of the firm of Hohner of Trossingen, who have exported mouth organs of many types and sizes to most parts of the world. Buschmann was also the first developer of the accordion [232b], but the big popularity of this instrument did not come until the present century. Wheatstone's heptagonal concertina [203], however, which he patented in 1844, was quickly taken up as an instrument for touring soloists. It was featured by Giulio

Regondi in 1846, and later in the century Alexander Prince played works like the over-ture to *Tannhäuser* on the 'Duet System' concertina, which had a complete chromatic scale for each hand[14]. In less complicated forms these easily portable instruments with treble-cum-bass potential had immediate and widespread acceptance by urban artisans and country people. Arnold Bennett describes in his novel *Clayhanger* an evening in a public house in the eighteen-seventies when there was 'some concertina-playing, with a realistic imitation of church bells borne on the wind from a distance'. Late in the evening Mrs Offlow, a champion clog-dancer, 'happening to be on tour with her hus-band through the realms of her championship', performed a dance in short red-and-black velvet skirts, accompanied by her husband on the concertina[15].

Behind all these developments in existing instruments and inventions of new ones lay fundamental changes in the forms of public music-making. Performances by touring virtuosi, alone or backed up by other public favourites, became the norm under demo-cratic types of government. Orchestral concerts were generally organized on a series subscription basis by societies such as the Gewandhaus in Leipzig and the Philharmonic Society (since 1913 the Royal Philharmonic Society) of London. Conducting was becom-ing a separate professional activity. For the Philharmonic Society's first series of concerts in 1813 Clementi conducted at the piano, with Salomon, who had organized Haydn's London concerts, as leader; in 1820 Spohr conducted with a baton on his first visit to the Society, and thereafter the term 'conductor' was used in place of 'at the piano'. Military bands were supported by military or civil authority – supreme examples are the band of the *Garde Republicaine* and the *Harmonie nautique de la ville de Genève*. Brass bands in general were and are maintained in circumstances where the comparative technical ease of the instruments and the vigorous and exhilarating effect of the whole are important considerations, e.g., in industry, in evangelistic religious movements such as the Salvation Army, and later in the United States in high schools and universities. Except in the case of England, which had no permanent opera until this century, and of Wagner's opera house at Bayreuth, which was subscribed for and given to him person-ally, opera remained a state or city institution, with permanently established positions for singers and instrumentalists. Solo performers like Liszt, Thalberg, Paganini, Ole Bull, Ysaye and many others played to mass audiences in halls which presented players and instrument makers with acoustical conditions and problems of an entirely new order.

Both violin and piano design developed in the direction of heavier stringing, increased tension and bigger compass. The lengthening of the neck of the violin was accompanied by internal reinforcement through the use of a larger bass bar – the strip of wood which runs most of the length of the instrument under the lower strings; the piano was reinforced by a metal frame, which was first used in large grands. The small square was superseded as the normal domestic piano by the upright [211], though large squares continued to be made and used in America for many years after their European demise. In the previous century writing music for amateurs had been a normal part of most composers' activity. In the nineteenth century it became a specialized business, resulting in an enormous amount of music of a comparatively virtuosic but musically undemanding kind, designed solely for amateur pianists. Composers like Sydney Smith and Joseph Ascher turned out hundreds of salon pieces of this sort, which continued to be the mainstay of the domestic pianist's repertory until the first World War. The harmonium was more common, however, in circles where the chief use of the domestic keyboard instrument was to play and accompany hymns and sacred songs.

While the changes in such solo instruments as the piano, violin and flute were made primarily for the sake of the virtuosi, discoveries and refashionings in other wind and in brass instruments seem most often to have been motivated by the demands of military bands, which needed complete ensembles of instruments capable of playing a full repertory of concert music, original and arranged. It took the combined researches of many designers and makers to make possible such new musical phenomena as Wieprecht's enormous stable of players for the Prussian military music, the army bands of France and Belgium, the industrial brass bands in England, and the crack touring United States army and show bands conducted by Patrick Gilmore and John Philip Sousa, who formed his own band in 1892 and took it on a world tour in 1910. Alfred Novello, son of the founder of the London publishing firm, reported in 1847 for the readers of the firm's house journal, the *Musical Times*, on the beginnings of the industrial brass band movement in England:

Whilst at Leeds, we visited the Public Gardens, in which a large Temperance Festival was being held, according to annual custom, on Whit-Tuesday, and we were both surprised and gratified by the manner in which several brass and wind bands executed a variety of opera and other airs. We understood the performers to be almost all workmen in the factories, many of the mills having their own special band. It must be a great reward to those by whose exertions this growing musical

E

taste has been fostered, to have seen the intelligent faces of these orderly and happy mechanics, dancing to the excellent music of their companions.

We remember, some years since, hearing with delight one of the earliest of these mill bands, formed by the kindness and energy of a large machine-maker at Bury, in Lancashire. Circumstances caused the dispersion of his men; but the good seed has not been sown in vain, for in the various shops in which they have found work, they have carried their love of music with them, and have been the beginnings of many similar bands. In the large workshops of the Great Western Railway, at Swindon, a number of these very men have combined to make a most excellent orchestra, seconded by the liberality and encouragement which seems to pervade the Company's arrangements at this village, for the benefit, improvement, and amusement of their workmen[16].

The great usefulness and comparative ease of playing of the valved brass was the chief factor in their quick dissemination and ultimate wide distribution in many situations involving both large bands and smaller ensembles playing popular and functional music, from provincial orchestras to Spanish bull-fight bands. In the southern United States wind bands provided the outdoor music for funerals of substantial citizens, and it was in this context of playing for night-time haunts and daytime processions that the first trends towards jazz-playing techniques began.

In this century of multiplying industries and increasingly populous cities and towns there was a regular and flourishing outgrowth of massed performances by outsize orchestras, bands and choirs, held in mammoth exhibition halls or in local cathedrals or arenas. Wieprecht's demonstration performance for the Emperor Nicholas I of Russia in 1838 of a concert by the united bands of sixteen infantry and sixteen cavalry regiments with a total of a thousand wind-players and two hundred drummers showed what could be done by centralized authority. As a private venture, Berlioz's concert at the Paris Exhibition of 1844 when with seven sub-conductors he directed five hundred and twenty-two singers and five hundred players was just as noteworthy. His amazed audience heard the horn chorus in the overture to *Der Freischütz* played by twenty-four horns, the prayer from Rossini's *Moses* by twenty-five harps, and the trio in the Scherzo from Beethoven's Fifth Symphony by thirty-six double basses. Also on the programme were Berlioz's *Hymn to France* and a *Chant des Industriels* written by Adolphe Dumas and set to music by Dumas's brother-in-law, the obscure composer Amédée Méraux. After the

London Exhibition of 1851 the great glass palace erected by Paxton was moved to the suburbs; the music for the reopening ceremony, with one thousand seven hundred performers conducted by Costa, included the *Hallelujah* Chorus, in which the performers were joined by a 'new brass band of foreigners, conducted by Herr Schallehn, a foreigner'. The Crystal Palace was subsequently used for regular concerts as well as for mammoth affairs like the Handel Festivals and the unveiling in 1860 of a colossal statue of Mendelssohn during a Mendelssohn concert by three thousand performers under Costa[17]. In Germany and Austria the organization of local festivals began in 1810 when Spohr directed a festival orchestra of two hundred players in the principal church of Frankenhausen. Mendelssohn's oratorios *St Paul* (1839) and *Elijah* (1847 – its first performance anywhere was at the Birmingham Festival of the previous year) were given first continental performances of festival proportions with eight hundred to a thousand performers by the Society of the Friends of Music in Vienna[18].

The instrument whose mode of operation was most radically changed by nineteenth-century inventions was the large organ. Charles S. Barker invented in 1834 a 'Pneumatic Lever' to be used instead of the mechanical tracker action. From 1867 onwards his 'complete system for applying electricity' to large organs, which he first installed in new organs in France, was successfully applied in many installations, especially in England, Germany and America. In England some of the increasingly large organs (the Albert Hall organ, built in 1871, had four manuals and one hundred and eleven stops, and was said to be 'the grandest and most complete instrument in the world') were installed at public expense in the town halls of larger cities and were played by professional city organists. One of the earliest cities to do so may have been Birmingham, where it was reported in 1844:

> The Trustees of the Town Hall, have directed the Organ to be played once a week for the amusement of the working people, from half-past seven to nine. The admission to any part of the Hall is threepence. The selection of music has been from the works of Haydn, Handel, Mozart, and Beethoven, interspersed with popular airs, and was highly enjoyed by 4,500 persons who attended the first three evenings[19].

The Paris Exhibition of 1890 had an exotic exhibit in a Javanese *gamelan* orchestra, which includes many tuned percussion instruments of wood and metal, together with flute, rebab and zither. Its sounds so engaged Debussy that he consciously turned to account in his orchestral writing the scales and tone-colours of the *gamelan*, thus initiating a new stage of cultural transference from East to West which has had an important outcome in instrumentation in this century. Earlier instances of contact with musical cultures outside the main Western stream concern eastern European gypsy music and Spanish gypsy and folk music. Rumanian gypsy ensembles around the middle of the century used fiddle, panpipes, *cobza* (similar to a lute) and small cimbalon, or as a minimum at peasant parties fiddle and *cobza* or fiddle and cimbalon or two fiddles. Liszt transferred to the piano the characteristic tremolando effects of the cimbalon, while both he and Brahms mistook for Hungarian folk-tunes the gypsified czardas melodies and romances, which were a customary part of Hungarian gypsy music. Later in the century the gypsy players of eastern Europe gave up their traditional panpipes and *cobza* though keeping the cimbalon, in the large factory-made form which first appeared in the eighteen-seventies[20]. To the present day, however, the indigenous folk-music of eastern Europeans has continued to be played on bagpipes, fretted zithers and hurdy-gurdies as well as on more modern instruments. Spanish gypsy music (*cante hondo* and *flamenco*) is a musical genre in its own right, with its mingling, unique in European music, of melancholy and exaltation, and its hypnotically compelling rhythms. From Bizet's *Carmen* (1875) onwards, non-Spanish composers drew on its more obvious characteristics with varying success. The completely successful translation of the highly coloured Spanish gypsy music and the soberer Spanish folk-music was accomplished by native Spaniards, notably Granados and Albeniz. Much of their material was derived from the researches of the remarkable musicologist and folklorist Felipe Pedrell – an early and striking case of the direct effect of musical research on musical creation. Until these composers the style of Spanish keyboard music had changed little since the time of Scarlatti.

In the nineteenth century amateurs and those preparing to be professionals normally had the same methods of training and could have the same teacher. The methods of star performers were far more widely distributed than had been possible before the discovery of cheap paper-making and cheap printing about 1820. This led to printing of ample supplies of 'methods' and 'studies', while the emulation of virtuosi led to the formation of professional 'schools' of performance. The prestige and knowhow of the personal pupils who gathered about a virtuoso in his home conservatory or in the larger centres of his tours descended with little diminution of brightness to their pupils and pupils of pupils. The science of instrumentation was furthered by the provision by the conservatories of teaching of instruments with more specialized uses. Berlioz pointed out as serious defects in the Paris Conservatoire programme in 1846 the neglect of some techniques in violin playing, including pizzicato and harmonics, and the absence of classes in viola, bass clarinet, saxophone, ophicleide, tuba, *cornet-à-pistons* and percussion instruments. Progressiveness or conservatism in the French national institutions depended largely on the professor of the particular instrument; until late in the century, for example, official teaching in the Paris Conservatoire ignored the valve horn. Berlioz also thought the ideal conservatory should have a professor of musical history, who should not only teach and write but also illustrate his subject by adequate and authentic performances. In this he was ahead of most conservatory thinking today; even in universities, whose music faculties have the history of composition and performance as their main concern, provision is still rarely made for illustrating the history of instrumental music with something approaching the authentic sounds of the instruments for which it was written. Collecting and maintaining old instruments for actual use is still a relatively new idea. Private collectors since the sixteenth century were probably moved by the same impulse as Duke Alfonso II of Ferrara, who, as Bottrigari reported, preserved instruments whose forms were 'different from those in which they are usually made today'. Those who planned the splendid Paris Conservatoire collection in 1795 expressed the modern three-sided interest in organology when they provided for a 'collection of antique or foreign instruments, and also for those in present-day use which by their perfection may serve as models'[21]. Since then many private collectors and some officials of public institutions have developed scientific methods of preserving, classifying and displaying musical instruments, viewing them as important evidence of man's social and artistic history. Frequently private collections have passed to public institutions. The Instrumental Museum of the Brussels Conservatoire, for example, was begun in 1872 with the purchase of Fétis's collection of Western and non-Western instruments. It received in 1876 the gift of a private collection of Indian instruments, and later acquired other private collections by gift and purchase. V.-C. Mahillon, member of a Brussels family of wind-instrument makers, who was curator from 1876 to his death in 1924, developed the collection into one of the largest in Europe, and also worked out a system of classifying instruments of every time and place which with refinements has been widely adopted.

The publication of accurate and complete, or nearly complete, editions of much pre-nineteenth-century music preceded by some time the awakening of interest in its authentic sonorities; 'practical' editions made from these sources were regularly turned out in unsuitably romantic guise. Wanda Landowska as virtuoso harpsichordist and writer and Arnold Dolmetsch as maker of and enthusiast for viols, lutes, recorders and keyboard instruments were almost alone in their generation in pursuing the more authentic re-creation of the music of the sixteenth to eighteenth centuries. The effect of their pioneering has been much greater on mid-twentieth-century musicology and performance than it was on their contemporaries, though in England, at least, harpsichords and early pianos were being restored for some cathedral organists as early as the eighteen-eighties.

1 E.Legouvé, *Sixty Years of Recollections*, trans. A.D.Vandam, i, 1893, p. 217.

2 We have used *Mémoires de Hector Berlioz*, 2 vols., Paris, n.d. (c 1920); there is an English translation *Memoirs of Hector Berlioz* (1935) revised by Ernest Newman from the earlier translation by R. and E.Holmes.

3 R.Morley Pegge, *The French Horn*, 1960, pp. 30–2.

4 Ibid., p. 40.

5 *Tristan und Isolde*, small score, 1904–5, p. vii.

6 *The Quarterly Musical Magazine and Review*, ix, 1827, pp. 76, 260.

7 Quoted in A.Baines, *Woodwind Instruments and their History*, 1962, p. 318.

8 F.G.Rendall, *The Clarinet*, 1954, pp. 92–4.

9 Ibid., pp. 102–3.

10 P.Bate, *The Oboe*, 1956, pp. 59–71.

11 R.Morley Pegge, 'The Horn, and later Brass', in *Musical Instruments through the Ages*, ed. A.Baines, 1961, pp. 311–14.

12 Rendall, pp. 147–55.

13 H.G.Farmer, *Military Music*, 1950, p. 62.

14 J.Howarth, 'Free-Reed Instruments', in *Musical Instruments through the Ages*, pp. 318–26.

15 A.Bennett, *Clayhanger* (Penguin Books, 1954), pp. 84–7.

16 P.A.Scholes, *The Mirror of Music*, i, 1947, p. 497.

17 Ibid., pp. 197, 420.

18 *Die Musik in Geschichte und Gegenwart*, s.v. 'Feste und Festspiele'.

19 Scholes, ii, pp. 587–91.

20 A.L.Lloyd, 'Play Gypsy!', *Audio and Record Review*, 1961, No. 4, p. 22.

21 *Die Musik in Geschichte und Gegenwart*, s.v. 'Instrumentensammlungen'.

9 Reproduction, mass production and cultural interchange 1918 onwards

Mechanical instruments and their history have not been included in the scope of this book. The modern science of the mechanical reproduction of specific musical performances, however, is without doubt the most influential single factor in the history and use of instruments since the end of the first World War. Earlier mechanical instruments such as the barrel organ, musical clocks and snuff-boxes, Debain's mechanical piano invented about 1850, and the Italian street 'organs', which were actually handle pianos, were all methods of providing, quite impersonally as well as mechanically, the sounds of musical pieces. The development of the phonograph and graphophone by Thomas Edison and others from 1887 onwards, and the devising in 1904 of a reproducing action for the previously mechanical player piano, made it possible to reproduce more or less faithfully the performances of named artists. Though reasonably successful for single performers or small groups, pre-electrical recording for the gramophone was imperfect for large instrumental ensembles, except perhaps military bands, with which many early recordings of standard works were made. During a relatively short life the pianola was much more highly regarded for its musical possibilities than the gramophone record by such famous pianists as Leschetizky, who was sorry it had not appeared a century earlier, and Busoni, who thought it as important as the cinematograph. The agonizing ordeal which recording for the gramophone could be for performers of their generation was graphically described by Busoni in a letter to his wife in November, 1919:

> . . . My suffering over the toil of making gramophone records came to an end yesterday, after playing for 3½ hours! I feel rather better today, but it is over. Since the first day, I have been as depressed as if I were expecting to have an operation. To do it is stupid and a strain. Here is an example of what happens. They want the Faust Waltz (which lasts a good ten minutes) *but it was only to take four minutes*! That meant quickly cutting, patching and improvising, so that there should still be some sense in it; watching the pedal (because it sounds bad); thinking of certain notes which had to be stronger or weaker in order to please this devilish machine; not letting oneself go for fear of inaccuracies and being conscious the whole time that every note was going to be there for eternity; how can there be any question of inspiration, freedom, swing or poetry? Enough that yesterday for 9 pieces of 4 minutes each (half an hour in all) I worked for three and a half hours! Two of these pieces I played four or five times. Having to think so quickly at the same time was a severe effort. In the

end, I felt the effects in my arms; after that, I had to sit for a photograph, and sign the discs.—At last it was finished! . . .

In 1922, just before he gave his last public concert at the age of fifty-six, Busoni wrote from his London hotel to his English manager that he was quite unable to face a proposed re-recording session:

> . . . Of course if the gramophone People insist on repeating the records, I will have to do it some time . . . I do not see the probability that the records should improve by repeating; the new ones may prove just as little 'satisfactory' as the original ones. And then? Had we to begin over again a third time?
>
> The conditions are most unfavourable. The room, the piano, the chair not inviting. I have to start like a race-horse and to end before four minutes have elapsed. I have to manage the touch and the pedal differently from how I do it usually.
>
> What, in heavens name!, can be the result of it? Not my own playing, take it for granted! Please consider the objections seriously and put them before Mr Brooks (I think this is the name of the 'recording Manager').

While some part of Busoni's revulsion at the indignity of the recording routine was probably due to the illness from which he died two years later, it nevertheless illuminates the revolution in concepts of performance which was begun by the gramophone and completed by talkies and television. Something of the drastic nature of the changed relationship between composer, performer and public which reproduction has entailed may be judged from the estimate of Busoni as an interpreter by a world-famous pianist born in this century, Claudio Arrau (*b* 1903):

> Busoni was not an interpreter in the sense we understand it. His main concern was not with interpreting a composer's intent. Very often the composer was almost totally lost. And even in those days Busoni was heavily criticized for it, particularly in Germany. Would we be able to accept such playing to-day? I think yes, if someone came along with a similar overpowering personality. This man was blessed with a wealth of creativity and an imagination of such grandeur and magnitude as to make everything he played a fascinating and mesmerizing experience. The Hammerklavier was gigantic and overwhelming but it was not Beethoven. Mozart was not Mozart but something miraculously rewoven. Busoni truly re-created – not in the

sense of re-creating something already created but in the sense of re-creating something totally new[1].

The situation which was such an ordeal to Busoni has become a commonplace routine for the top performers of Arrau's generation, who may often have in one day a morning rehearsal, an afternoon recording session and an evening concert. Since the ideal requirements of performance in a recording studio are complete predictability and total accuracy – however exacting, technically and emotionally, the music may be – the effect has been to alter the balance in the personality of the performing artist in favour of the virtuoso technician as against the creative interpreter. The introduction of electrical recording with microphone in 1924 (which made it possible to record acceptably large ensembles of instruments of many different tone-colours) was followed by sound films in the early nineteen-thirties and the widespread use of magnetic recording (tape-recording) and the coming of television since the second World War. These have effected a basic change in the lives of the great body of professional instrumentalists in the large centres of mechanical reproduction. Recording puts a premium not only on the utter dependability of the performer but also on the complete certainty of behaviour of his instrument; hence the French bassoon has been largely displaced by the Heckel bassoon [222a, b], and the small-bore horn customary in France by the large-bore German-type horn [224b], even though these changes have involved a considerable loss of instrumental individuality. Similarly, trends in the design of brass and wind instruments have been in the direction of greater ease of emission, while the saxophone has had a radical redesigning both of bore and fingering system at the hands of M. Charles Houvenaghel of the Paris firm of Leblanc [221].

Sound reproduction has also wrought basic changes in the pattern of employment of professional instrumentalists, particularly in large cities. The varying methods of running a complex professional machine which have been adopted by the different countries of Europe and the North American continent have made for greater diversity between the working conditions of instrumentalists than ever before. In Moscow the state employs nearly every professional player, while in Berlin and Paris a minority hold life-positions from the city or state and the remainder are largely freelance. In London the membership of the B.B.C.'s orchestras and of the orchestra of the Covent Garden Opera House is relatively stable, while that of the other orchestras may vary with each concert or recording engagement, according to the availability of a roster of players and the inclination of the 'fixer' (the orchestra's official for booking players)[2]. In an earlier stage of their history orchestras in the United States were mainly supported and virtually owned by a few wealthy families (Henry L. Higginson paid the Boston Symphony's annual deficit of some fifty thousand dollars from 1881 until 1918). Today each of the twenty-four 'major' orchestras – those which contract with their musicians on a per-season basis and whose annual budget is at least two hundred and fifty thousand dollars – is a prestige-symbol of its city's prosperity and maturity, and is supported by a cross-section of its citizens, business firms and other organizations. In 1958–9 the Los Angeles Philharmonic Orchestra had 3,500 contributors, the Cincinnatti Symphony 17,300[3]. In places where reproduction industries are heavily concentrated, changes in the pattern of employment of instrumentalists may be swift. Los Angeles, for example, was a mecca for instrumentalists until the recent drastic reduction in the demand for large-scale orchestral music, due both to the decline of the film industry and to the trend towards smaller and less standardized ensembles for film and television music. For these reasons the market in America and Britain for one-instrument players, even of a good standard, is less, while for those who can deal competently with two, three or even more instruments, particularly woodwind, it is greater.

After 1918, the rise of the orchestra in the United States was closely accompanied by a decline in city and community bands, and the end of the triumphs of such band-conductors as Gilmore, Sousa and Victor Herbert, who was for a time Gilmore's successor as director of the Twenty-Second Regiment Band, becoming conductor of the Pittsburg Symphony Orchestra in 1898. After the first World War the bands of the U.S. Army and Navy took the place of the regimental bands, while the fashionable resorts dropped bands in favour of dance orchestras. The Edwin Franko Goldman Band, however, was founded in New York in 1911, and still continues as a notable professional band. The big development of the period in the United States was the rapid growth of bands in schools, colleges and universities, where the massive grandeur of their sound and the relative playing-ease of the instruments make them particularly suitable for football games and academic ceremonial on a large scale. The rapid development since the end of the second World War of the lower clarinets [220] has contributed considerably to this expansion, and the success of the bass and contra-bass clarinets has resulted in a dramatic decline in the use of bassoons. Modern methods of mass production [216, 217] have enabled manufacturers to meet the enormously increased demands of bands, and to a lesser degree of orchestras, in educational institutions[4]. In England a comparably rapid development of instrumental music in schools and a resulting increase in the demand for cheap instruments have followed the passing of the Education Act of 1945. The time-honoured craft methods must nevertheless still be used for many of the highest-grade professional instruments [214, 215].

Gramophone records were the first mass disseminators of many kinds of music outside the areas in which they were indigenous. Music which would remain alien on one hearing soon became familiar through repetition. A striking example is the dissemination of the spontaneous, highly emotional and essentially improvisatory manner of performance of authentic jazz in the nineteen-twenties. Authentic jazz is the only known case of a completely original timbre, impulse and whole musical ethos produced on instruments with a formal tradition of quite another kind. Apart from the considerable musical influence of jazz, the extraordinary technical achievements of the greatest jazz instrumentalists have widened the bounds of accepted technical competence on many instruments, particularly percussion and wind. The high-register playing of the best jazz trumpeters is the only contemporary brass technique to compare with the specialized *clarin* playing of the Bach era. A 'hybrid' form of jazz, mainly for ballroom dancing of the Foxtrot, Black Bottom, Charleston and so on, was already widespread in the late twenties, partly through the gramophone. 'At the tailend of the twenties, however, we observe', says Francis Newton, 'the tiny beginnings of an expansion of the thoroughbred jazz among small obscure and untypical communities in Europe, and to a much lesser extent, in America. The imported gramophone records of white New York musicians, and later of the great coloured players, were almost entirely responsible – in Europe at least – for the creation of these small groups of devotees'[5]. In Paris in the early thirties this authentic improvisatory jazz was transmuted into French terms by the *Quintette du Hot-Club de France*, a combination of the genius gypsy guitarist Django Reinhardt and the brilliant violinist Stephane Grappelly with a rhythm section of two guitars and a string bass. The world-wide distribution of records has also been the main factor in a two-way traffic of musical styles and practices between European and non-European societies. In some cases there is a complete transference, as with the Western-style Tokyo Symphony Orchestra, with Professor Mantle Hood's Eastern ensembles at the Institute of Ethnomusicology at the University of California in Los Angeles, and with the steel band played by members of one of the bands of Her Majesty's Brigade of Guards at a reception for the West Indian cricket team. In other cases indigenous Eastern music is played on Western instruments, as with the Official Ensemble of the Chinese People's Republic, which performs with Chinese and Western instruments. In still other cases the meeting of East and West has resulted in the mingling in varying proportions of both musical styles and instruments; in Turkey, for example, European clarinet and Turkish psaltery may be found in the same ensemble, while in Egypt one may find playing together the European violin and the Egyptian *nay*, the ancient open-ended flute. The take-over by the West of percussion and tuned percussion from Latin America and the Caribbean (e.g., marimbas, maracas, scrapers and bongos) was first for performances of exotic music like the *rumba*, and later as normal components of many ensembles. A welcome and completely successful new departure in instruments for education is the use of tuned percussion specially designed for playing by children [228, 248]. A striking case of the acceptance by extra-Europeans of European mass-produced instruments is the great success of the cheap guitar in negro Africa, where it is played with consummate expertise and style. In the parts of the New World where the Spanish conquerors remained as settlers the chief instruments transplanted from Europe were guitar, violin, harp, *chirimia* (shawm) and organ. In much of South America the harp continues to be played in virtually its seventeenth-century form. Latin-American popular ensembles consisting of this robust harp with guitars and singers have had great success in Europe in both live and recorded performance. An intriguing instance of modern 'revival' is that of the Janissary Band in Turkey. Created in 1320 for Sultan Orhan with at first sixty-six and later seventy-seven players, this was suppressed in 1826 and reconstituted in slightly modernized form in 1923 as a *folklorique* feature of the Turkish army.

The widening of musical horizons historically as well as geographically has been one of the chief characteristics of instrumental knowledge and practice in this century. The performances of Landowska and Dolmetsch were posited from the start on the resumption of the making of earlier types, initially of harpsichord, clavichord, viols, lute and recorder. Landowska played harpsichords by the Paris firm of Pleyel, who pioneered the modern harpsichord with iron frame; Dolmetsch set up his workshop for making keyboards, strings and recorders at Haslemere in 1914 after supervising harpsichord-making at Chickering's in Boston and at Gaveau's in Paris. Since 1918 the demand has steadily increased, especially for harpsichord and clavichord, with a corresponding growth in the number and distribution of makers. Making of wind instruments, except the recorder, has developed slowly. The reason for this is that the more immediately playable instruments of the Baroque era have been from the outset the basis of the 'revival'.

There is good reason why this should be the case with keyboard instruments, including the organ, in which modern forms of Baroque tonal ideas have been conspicuously successful [226, 245]. However, even with the Baroque period the nature of woodwind and brass instruments has been explored only comparatively recently. The cornett, most difficult of all wind instruments but much used in pre-Baroque times for its sweetness and singing quality, is only now beginning to be made [243] and played. At the other end of the scale the recorder [234], which is cheap to make and has been greatly promoted in education, is made chiefly in the post-Hotteterre form, which is easier to play but emasculated in tone compared with the pre-Baroque large-bore recorder. Medieval instruments and instrumental practices are still under-explored territory; in default of serious research the unhistorical procedure has too often been followed of projecting our ideas about Baroque instruments and instrumental functions back into earlier centuries. Often so-called medieval-type instruments are made on the slimmest visual evidence and using later and irrelevant constructional methods. Artificial amplification has been accepted for many years on the electric guitar. In fact it has led to changes in the instrument's form, as it has in the for-thrumming-only double bass, which now sometimes appears as nothing more than a long, shallow box with a neck and four strings. Amplification of harpsichord and clavichord tone, however, is a subject which arouses bitter controversy, being regarded from one viewpoint as essential, and from another as immoral.

In a small number of the many institutions where surviving instruments from earlier times are collected and preserved, care is also taken to keep them in playing order [241], and in some cases to make them available to responsible performers. It is impossible, however, that there can be enough surviving instruments to provide for all performances of the music which requires them, and the manufacture of *historische Instrumenten*, as present-day forms of earlier instruments are called in Germany, is now a considerable business[6], with a large amateur market.

Apart from the vibraphone [229], the only significant newly invented instruments in the twentieth century are those in which the sound is produced wholly by electronic means. One of the earliest essays was the theremin, invented by a Russian of that name and demonstrated in 1920. This is a melodic instrument whose pitch is controlled by movements of the player's hand in relation to an antenna. None of the considerable number of electronic instruments which have been invented – they include the *Ondes Martenot* (which Messiaen used in the score of his *Turangalila*), the trautonium and the electronde – has made more than the slightest ripple on the surface of musical practice, with the exception of the electronic organ. This instrument has made a place for itself in circumstances where ease of maintenance and appeal to the amateur player are of most concern. (There is a parallel here with the early history of the pianoforte.) The following is quoted in its entirety from a newspaper item headed 'Boom in Organs':

One Oxford music shop reports a boom in the sale of electronic organs – which cost between £250 and £600, are easier to play than pianos, about the same size, and require no tuning.

People who learnt to play the piano at school, and then gave it up for 30 or 40 years, seem to be the buyers. 'Using very few fingers, you can produce a remarkable number of effects, and play the same tune in many different ways,' said Mr Trevor Taphouse, who first played an electronic organ at St Michael's Church in 1938.

The click of a switch produces 'cathedral tone', complete with echo, there are string tones and triangle tones, church bell effects and a realistic xylophone noise.

Thoughtfully, the makers of several models provide a 'soft-play' switch, so you could play it in the flat at midnight—even cathedral tone.

Why not lay your car up for the winter and buy yourself an electronic organ? But be warned—Mr Taphouse says that if you have no musical sense, you will not find any more satisfaction with one of these than with a piano[7].

Behind the development of electronic sound for musical purposes there lies a vast programme of research in the sound-reproduction industry. One of the most complicated pieces of apparatus constructed for research in all aspects of specified sound and its reproduction [247] has recently been put at the disposal of a group of composers interested in its creative use. In many other places also composers are experimenting in the possibilities of tape recording for realizing arrangements of sounds whose original mode of production is not revealed to the listener.

Outside sophisticated urban centres people in many parts of Europe still keep to musical habits whose origins lie far back in history. Some are extremely ancient practices, like the Cretan shepherds' playing on open-ended flutes made of bird's wing-bone. Others are survivals from the Middle Ages, like the folk-fiddling in Scotland and Scandinavia, and the little bands of bagpipe, bowed string, drum and open-ended flute in the Balkans, or decayed baroque, like the playing of 'sonatas' on pipe and tabor after the Epistle and at other points in the Mass in certain remote churches in the Balearics. There are mixtures of medieval and modern, such as the Auvergne ensembles of bag-pipe, hurdy-gurdy and accordion, and the massing together of originally solo instru-ments, like the bands of *épinettes* in the Vosges and of pipes and tabors in the Basque country. When Pope Pius X, in his *Motu Proprio* of 1903, forbade bands in church, and permitted wind instruments 'only in special cases with the consent of the Ordinary', it is likely that he had in mind the Haydn-Mozart tradition of church music in Austria rather than the playing, still current in Asturias, of bagpipes after the Elevation of the Host at a fiesta Mass, or of a band of saxophones and clarinets followed shortly by a competing bagpipe in a church procession.

Many folk instruments have gone from Europe to America, in earlier times with colonizers, as did the partly fretted zithers to the Appalachians, and later with immi-grants, as did for example the *tamburitza* bands from Yugoslavia to New York. Within the past decade there has been a strong movement in the opposite direction of the instru-mental styles of the country music of the rural south of the United States – a complex mixture of negro and white elements, done with cheap instruments such as guitar, banjo and harmonica. Becoming popular in America outside its natural context, it has been commercialized and has had widespread influence on the style of presentation of folk and popular song in Europe and urban America. While folk and popular songs accompanied with guitar go back very far in southern Europe, the present wave of popularity of this *genre* of accompaniment in English-speaking countries must be con-sidered a development from the North American source, disseminated in the first place by recordings, as was authentic jazz.

In countries where Western commerce is less effective or does not penetrate, the state takes a purposeful hand in the conservation and official presentation of folk material – again out of its natural context. This is done partly with folk instruments and partly with 'art' instruments, in Greece, Hungary, Rumania, Bulgaria, the various regions of Yugoslavia, and the many republics of the Soviet Union, all of which maintain official touring groups of dancers, singers and instrumentalists.

The history of music and the history of musical instruments depend on sources which sometimes overlap but frequently diverge. Written and printed notes are a major material of the history of music, in the sense of the history of musical design, of counter-point and of harmony – elements in which the formal manifestations of European musical activity are traceable. A history of instruments which relied mainly on written music would give a very myopic view (or rather a very 'myaural' hearing) of its subject. Instruments are physical things, and their history is to be written in the physical terms of their making and working. Ultimately they are also objects as functional as clothes or houses, and are an equally inseparable part of social behaviour. Written music, again, can say very little about the magic triangle of relationship between maker, player and occasion of performance. The activity of a man with a tin whistle playing to a waiting queue outside a concert hall can tell us as much as that of a man with a Stradivarius who is about to play inside it. As Madeau Stewart has put it:

> Differences between one sort of music and another are proliferated and emphasized to the degree that we believe in them. In fact there are only two sorts of music: written and unwritten. For the rest, music is music is music[8].

Today there is every sign that the inter-continental and inter-cultural traffic which the twentieth century has so far seen will increase. While the eventual results are as unpredictable as were those of the medieval mixture of Arab and northern European traditions, the predominance of the present forms of European instrumental traditions in the inevitable mingling with African, Far and Near Eastern and North and South American is by no means to be assumed.

1 *Recorded Sound* (Journal of the British Institute of Recorded Sound, 38 Russell Square, W.C.1), i (8), 1962, pp. 279, 256–8, facsimiles between pp. 254–5. Busoni's letters are quoted from *Letters to His Wife* by Ferrucio Busoni, translated by R.Ley, by courtesy of Edward Arnold (Publishers) Ltd., and from the facsimiles by courtesy of Mrs Emmy Tillett and the British Institute of Recorded Sound.

2 Peter Heyworth, 'The Concert Crisis', *The Observer*, November 10, 1963.

3 Helen M.Thompson, 'The American Symphony Orchestra', *One Hundred Years of Music in America*, 1961, pp. 36–52.

4 R.F.Goldman, 'Band Music in America', ibid., pp. 128–39.

5 F.Newton, *The Jazz Scene*, 1959, pp. 63–4.

6 See the 'Provisional Index of Present-day Makers of Historical Musical Instruments (Non-Keyboard)', with a 'Provisional List of Makers of Historical Keyboard Instruments', *Galpin Society Journal*, xiii, 1960, p. 70.

7 *The Oxford Mail*, November 13, 1963.

8 Madeau Stewart, 'A Music in Peril', *Audio and Record Review*, May, 1963, p. 67.

Illustrations

Prehistory

1

2

3

1 Cave painting, *c* 10,000–15,000 B.C., showing a human figure disguised in a bison skin pursuing two horned animals. The object held to the masked mouth of the figure has been interpreted as a musical bow or a bone flute. *Les Trois Frères, Ariège*

2 Two single-note whistles, *c* 10,000 B.C., from La Madeleine and Langerie Basse. They are made from reindeer phalanges, whose natural notch directs the player's breath against the man-made hole. *Pitt Rivers Museum, Oxford*

3 Fipple flute with three finger-holes, made from the tibia of a roe deer (the fipple is missing). It was found near Vesterbølle in Jutland inside a pre-Roman Iron Age jar. *Jutland Archaeological Society*

4 Two single-note fipple whistles made from willow stems. The fipples are clearly visible above the roughly cut 'windows'. These whistles are made by German boys in springtime. *Pitt Rivers Museum, Oxford*

5 Two small vertical open-ended flutes made from crane's wing-bone. The smaller decorated example is from Egina, the larger is from Samos. *Pitt Rivers Museum, Oxford*

6 Kaval from Herzegovina. This vertical open-ended flute of decorated wood is a folk survival of the ancient open-ended flute. Although the construction of these flutes is simple, the technique of playing is extremely difficult. *Pitt Rivers Museum, Oxford*

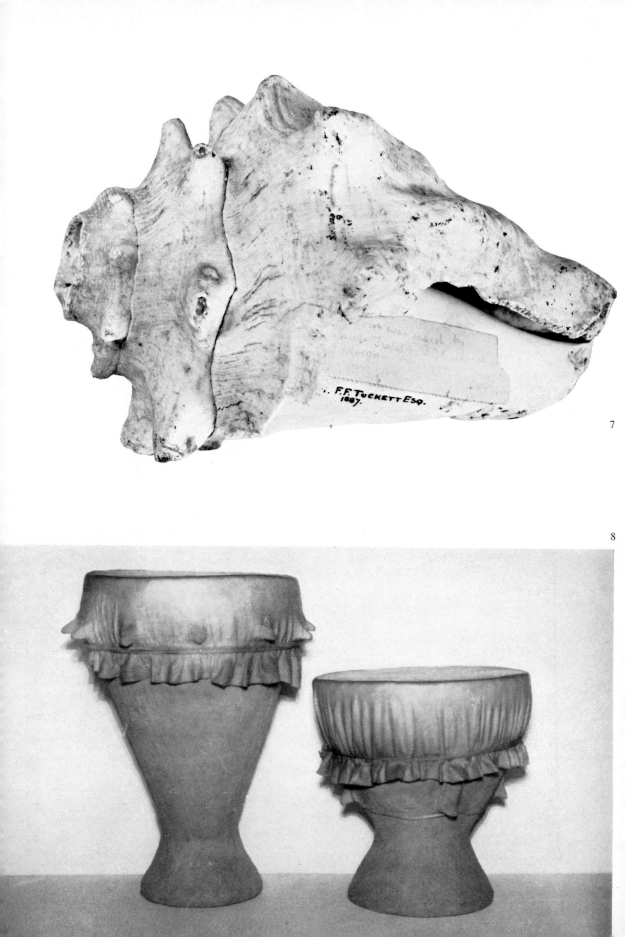

7

8

7 Conch-shell, the most primitive trumpet prototype. This shell was used for many years as a fog signal at sea by a 19th-century Cornish fisherman, Joseph Tresize.
Pitt Rivers Museum, Oxford

8 Reconstructions of hand-built clay drums of *c* 2000 B.C., found in fragments at Kralupy and Brozany in Bohemia. Drums of wheel-turned pottery are still widely used in Africa, the Balkans and the East.
Original fragments, National Museum, Prague: reconstructions by Isabel Shaw

9 Clay friction drum from Naples, used at the Fiesta of the Madonna of Piedigrotta. The small squeaker shown beside it, and a conch-shell trumpet similar to that in plate 7, are also played at this fiesta.
Pitt Rivers Museum, Oxford

10 Three small friction drums: *La Cocotte*, a cardboard fairground toy from Puy de Dôme; a Norwegian example made from a tailor's thimble with a horsehair friction thread; and a mustard-tin drum from Norwich. *Pitt Rivers Museum, Oxford*

9

10

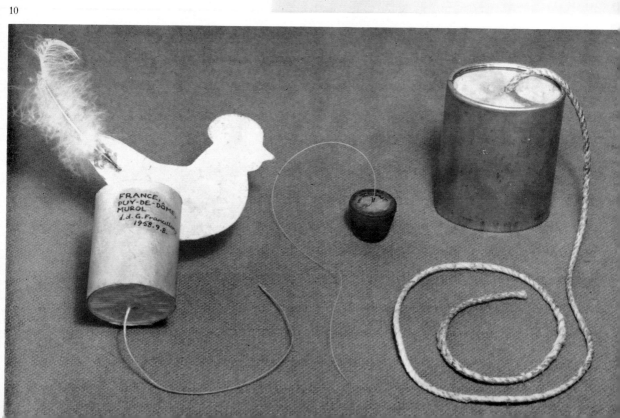

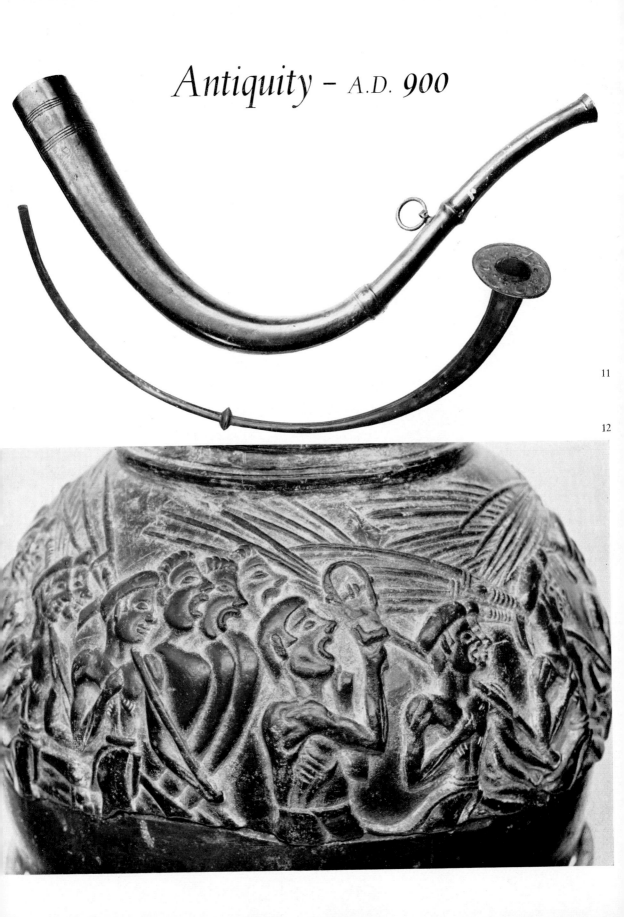

11

12

1 Irish bronze 'horns'. Bronze Age instruments of horn-
and trumpet-like character existed in several forms.
That above is related to the plainly curved animal
horn; that below is a large semicircular trumpet of
the kind which was possibly played in pairs on ceremonial occasions.   *National Museum of Ireland, Dublin*

2 A *sistrum*, or metal frame rattle, is shaken by the leader
of this group of singing harvesters, depicted on a
Cretan steatite vessel from Haga Triada; *c* 1550–1500 B.C.
The 'Harvester' Vase   *Candia Museum, Crete*

3 Two bronze rattles, generally called crotals by archae-
ologists, though they bear no relation to the *krotala* of
antiquity. These instruments have been found only
in Ireland and Wales; there are, however, late neolithic pottery prototypes from eastern Europe.
    National Museum of Ireland, Dublin

4 Three dancers with *krotala*, or wooden clappers; *c* 540
B.C. Spanish castanets are the most familiar present-
day example of dancers' self-accompanying instruments.
Greek neck amphora   *Ashmolean Museum, Oxford*

13

14

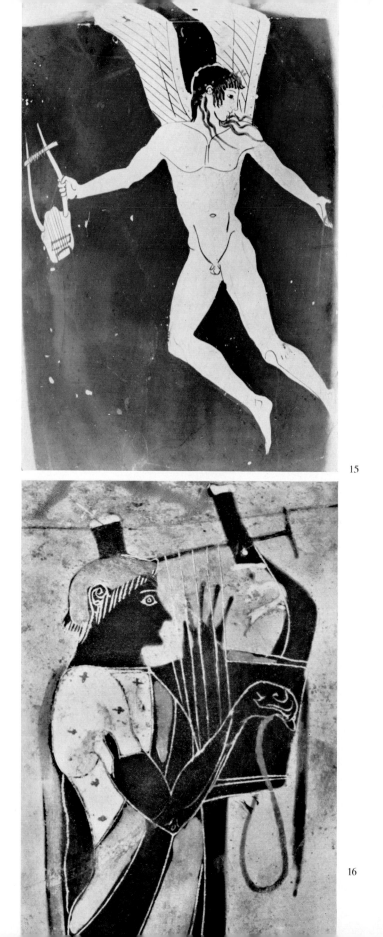

15

16

17

18

15 A flying Eros carrying a lyre; *c* 470 B.C. In modern terminology, *lyre* is generally taken to mean this simple form of the most common Greek stringed instrument.
Red figured lethykos from Gela
Ashmolean Museum, Oxford

16 Apollo playing a *kithara*; *c* 600 B.C. This was a larger and more elaborately constructed instrument of the same basic type as the lyre. The plectrum is in Apollo's right hand.
Greek neck amphora   *Berlin Antiquarium*

17 Cylindrical cane pipe with up-cut single reed and two finger-holes, from Cyprus. This most primitive form of reed instrument, with a reed cut from the body of the tube itself and therefore not renewable, is practical only if the player makes his own instrument.
Pitt Rivers Museum, Oxford

18 Greek double aulos, *c* 450 B.C., here played during preparations for the Feast of Dionysus. This was the developed form of cylindrical reed instrument with large lip-controlled double reeds.
Red figured stamnos from Gela
Ashmolean Museum, Oxford

19 The Elgin *auloi*, 5th century B.C., were found with lyre fragments in a tomb near Athens. They are warped and shrunk with age and no reeds survived with them.
British Museum, London

19

EX·DONO·DVCIS·SFORTIAE·SFORTIAE

20 *Kithara* (with plectrum), panpipes and double aulos, of which one pipe is broken, are played by Sirens on this Etruscan frieze of the 2nd century B.C.

Ashmolean Museum, Oxford

21 A bronze *lituus*, whose hooked shape is also found among Celtic bronze instruments, is carried by a figure in this Etruscan funeral scene, 4th century B.C., from the Tomb of the Monkey, Chiusi.

Archaeological Museum, Florence

22 Roman relief showing a eunuch high-priest of Cybele and instruments associated with her cult: *tympanon,* clapper cymbals and Phrygian aulos. The two pipes of the aulos (the larger with the upturned, horn-shaped end characteristic of the Phrygian variety) are here shown crossed over each other. Details of sectional construction are clearly visible, also the large reed on the shorter pipe. That on the larger pipe is damaged; 2nd century A.D.

Capitoline Museum, Rome

25

23 The signal of victory in a gladiatorial combat is accompanied by two *cornui*, or curved 'trumpets', a *tuba*, or straight trumpet, and a *hydraulis*, or water-powered organ; 1st century A.D.
Mosaic   *Zliten, Tripoli, Libya*

24 Roman street musicians, with *tibia* (double aulos), small cymbals and large *tympanon* or frame drum. Mosaic from Pompeii by Dioscorides of Samos; 1st century B.C.   *National Museum, Naples*

25 Small bronze cymbals, of the type shown in the mosaic in plate 24   *British Museum, London*

26 *Duduk* with damaged reed. Cylindrical pipes sounded with double reeds survive now only in the Caucasus and in Japan. The Caucasian duduks are played in pairs, but by two players, not one, as was the double aulos.   *Deutsches Museum, Munich*

27 One pipe of bone, part of a Roman tibia. This, like the pipes of the Phrygian aulos in plate 22, is constructed in several segments. The bore is cylindrical throughout, although the external dimensions vary.
Pitt Rivers Museum, Oxford

26   27

31

30

28 Sarcophagus showing a funeral banquet, with a tibia, and a long fingerboard stringed instrument which is not precisely identifiable by name in any Latin source   *Lateran Museum, Rome*

29 Latin Christian epitaph, 4th century A.D., showing the Good Shepherd with panpipes. This instrument had a long association with simple, rustic and pastoral pursuits, and unlike the reed and percussion instruments of pagan civilization was accepted in early Christian iconography.   *Vatican Museum*

30 Serbian double *frula* (a fipple flute), cut from one piece of wood. Rustic flutes of this kind also had no specific associations with pagan religion, and presumably escaped the strictures of the early Christian Fathers against musical instruments. The 'flute' of which the early Church so disapproved was not in fact a flute, but the aulos or tibia, whose name has been constantly mistranslated.   *Pitt Rivers Museum, Oxford*

31 Bosnian bagpipe. This is one of the simplest forms of bagpipe, droneless, and with a bag made from a whole skin.   *Pitt Rivers Museum, Oxford*

32

33

32 David with a nordic lyre; c A.D. 700. The lyre of antiquity, which vanished from its Mediterranean homelands, survived in robuster form among the Teutonic and Celtic peoples of northern Europe.
Canterbury Psalter   *British Museum*

33 David with a rudimentary 'lute'; c A.D. 850. Finger-board instruments, or news of them, seem to have begun to reach western Europe from Middle Eastern sources from the 9th century onwards. Early depictions are often somewhat unreliable in detail.
Lothair Psalter   *British Museum*

900–1300

34 Irish high cross, showing the Last Judgment; 10th century A.D. The blessed are on the left behind two musicians, one playing a short 'trump' and the other what appears to be an oblique lyre, on whose upper part a bird sits. The damned are on the right, herded by a devil with a trident, beside whom sits a figure playing a triple pipe.
East Face of Muiredach's Cross
                    Monasterboice, County Louth, Ireland

35 Organ; 12th century A.D. This rough depiction of the early medieval organ was derived from the 9th-century Utrecht Psalter, itself taken from an earlier Byzantine model.   Cambridge Psalter   *Trinity College, Cambridge*

36 Olifant from La Chartreuse de Portes; 11th century. These aristocratic signal horns, introduced from Byzantium in the 10th century, were elaborately and elegantly carved.   *Bibliothèque Nationale, Paris*

34

35

36

37

38

39a

37 David as a shepherd boy, playing panpipes; 11th century A.D. This shows again the innocent pastoral association of plate 29.
Psalter   *Ivrea Cathedral Library*

38 King David with attendant musicians; 11th century A.D. David's lyre is fanciful. The figure below him strikes with a plectrum a 'lute' in which pegs, frets on the fingerboard and perforations in the skin-covered belly are shown. To the right are a formalized organ and two supposedly Hebrew instruments.
Psalter   *Ivrea Cathedral Library*

39 Musician figures beside examples of melodies in the Gregorian modes; late 11th or early 12th century A.D. Bowed lyres developed probably in the 11th century; the Arab *kanun*, from which the European psalteries derived, was played in Muslim and probably in Christian Spain; panpipes were rustic instruments, and single and double cylindrical reed pipes may well have survived as such. The straight trumps and clappers seem to be taken from antique models, as does another figure (not given here) with cup-shaped cymbals.
Troparium, St Martial   *Bibliothèque Nationale, Paris*
a King David playing a bowed and fingered lyre
b A straight trump and clappers on long stems
c Panpipes
d Single reed pipe accompanying a juggler
e Double reed pipe accompanying a juggler
f Square psaltery with ten strings, probably intended to represent the 'instrument of ten strings' of the Psalms
g Horn and triangular psaltery

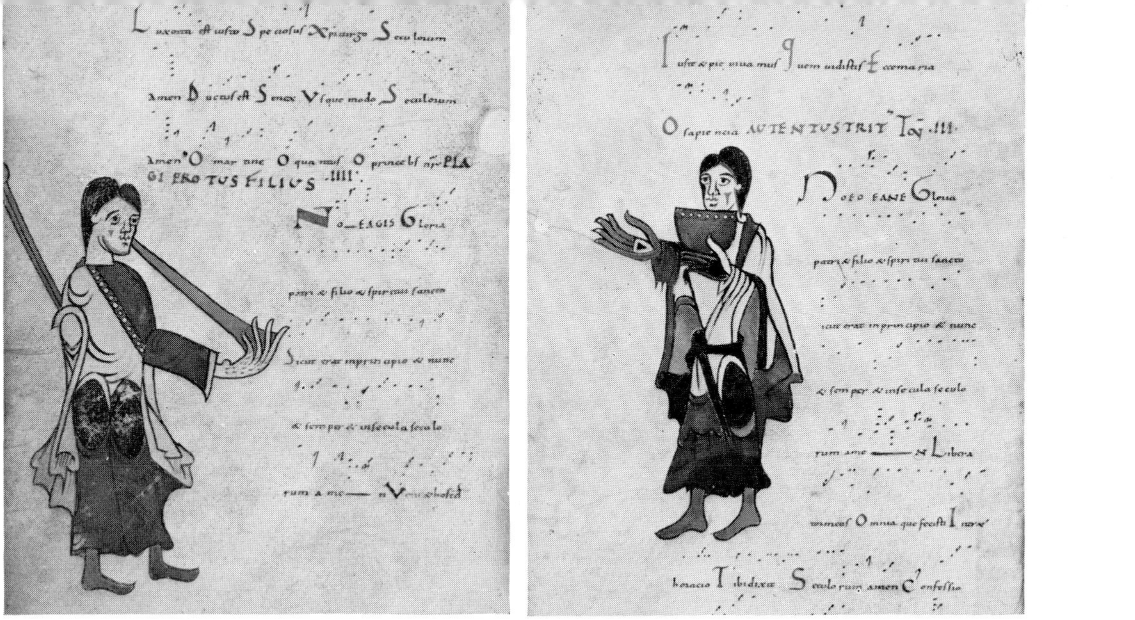

39*b*, *c*

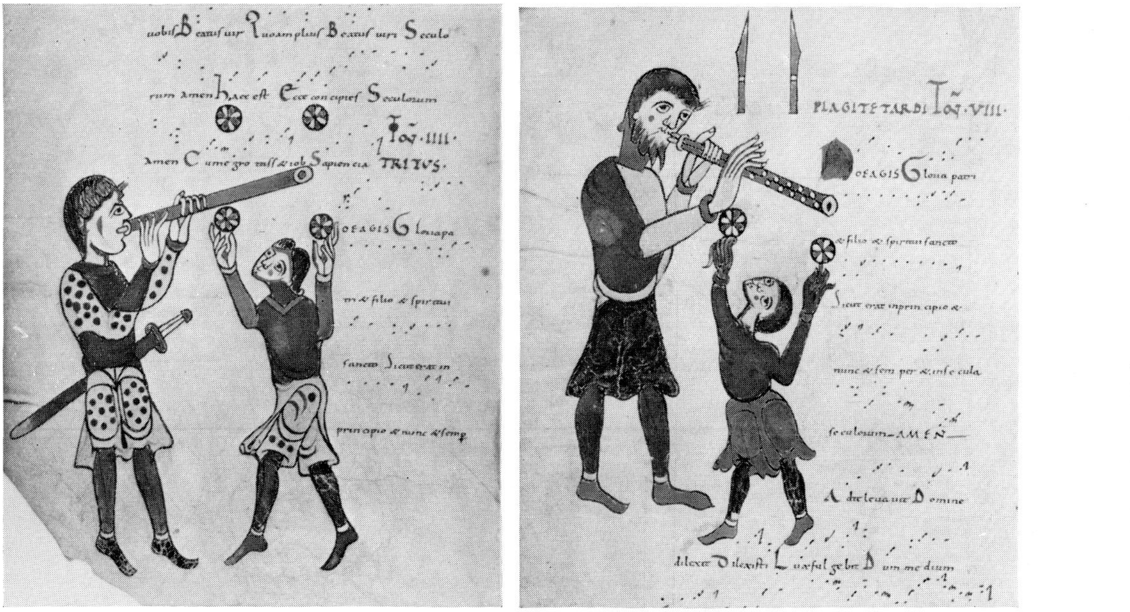

39*d*, *e*

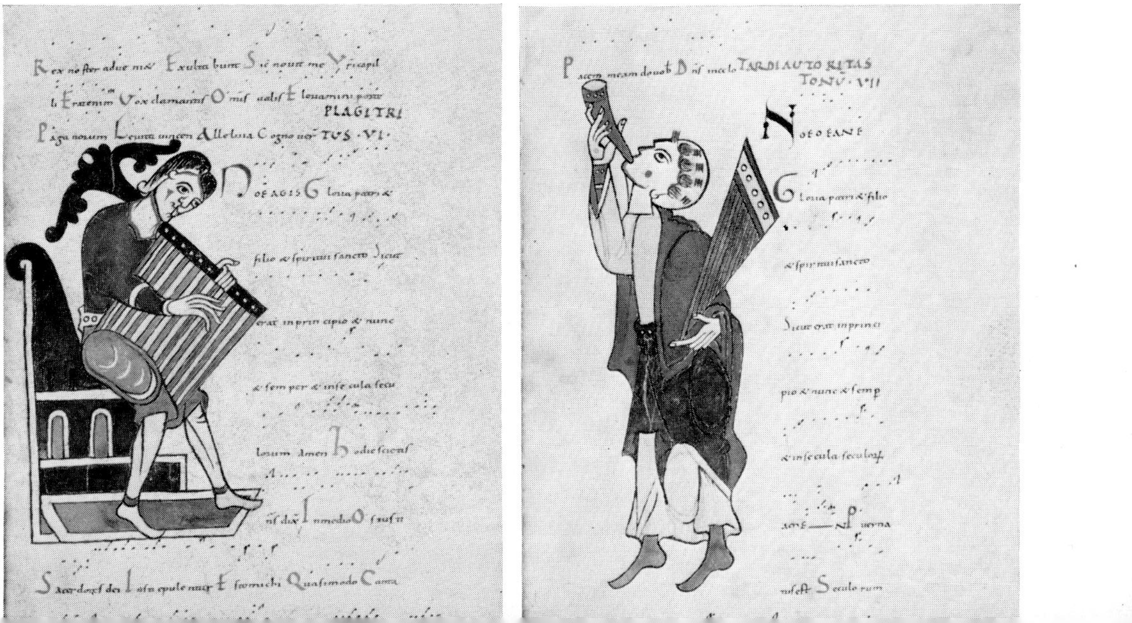

39*f*, *g*

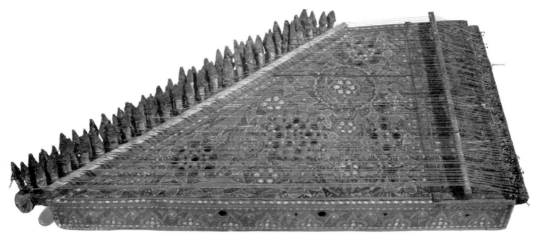

40

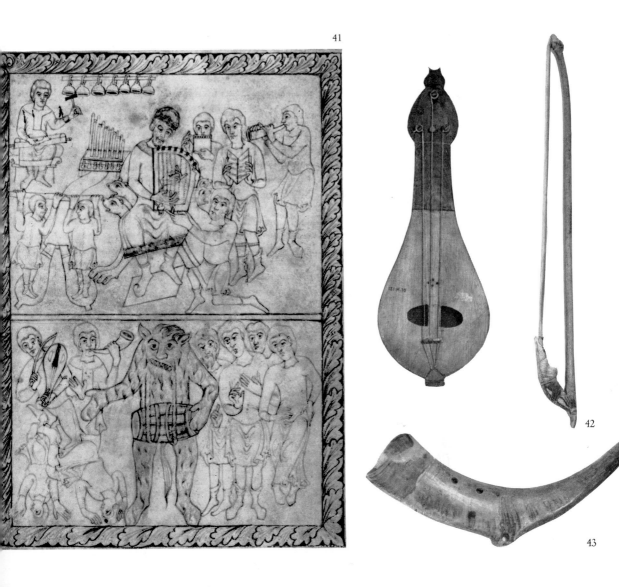

41

42

43

44

40 Arab *kanun*, modern form of the Middle Eastern zither from which the European psalteries derived.
Pitt Rivers Museum, Oxford

41 Sacred and profane music; 12th century. King David plays an inaccurately depicted harp; left are church and song-school instruments – an organ, tuned bells (*cymbala*) and a monochord; right is a singer with music book, and players of rustic instruments – panpipes and fingered horn. An animal figure playing a barrel drum, two tumblers and two jongleurs with unfingered horn and *lira* are shown below.
Psalter from the Abbey of St Remigius, Reims
St John's College, Cambridge

42 Greek *lira*. This folk instrument is essentially the same as that in plate 41, which had reached the West by the 11th century. *Pitt Rivers Museum, Oxford*

43 Jewish *shofar*, or fingered ram's horn, used to summon the faithful. Animal horns with finger-holes are played still by Scandinavian and Iberian shepherds.
Pitt Rivers Museum, Oxford

44 David tuning a harp, with representative musicians; 12th century. These are fairly exact depictions of song-school and secular instruments. The bells are arranged in two series. The left half ascends UT, RE, MI, FA, SOL, LA; the right half ascends similarly but starts from the right-hand end. The three bells in the middle are FA (B♭), MI (B♮) with an unnamed bell in between, which would be called either SOL or FA, according to the series by which it was approached. The figures below David play secular instruments – four-stringed *lira* and three-stringed fiddle held downwards – and rustic instruments – triple pipe, perhaps meant to represent panpipes, and bone fipple flute. The lower border figures play handbells, psaltery with quill plectra (the psaltery's double stringing is clearly shown), and organistrum. The handbell-player and the operator of the organistrum keys appear to be singing and these two groups may represent song-school rehearsal practice.
Hunterian Psalter *Glasgow University Library*

47

48

45 Player of three-stringed, short-necked oval fiddle, and dancing figure; late 12th century. This, rather than the large later instrument with five strings, is probably the *vièle* of the troubadours and early trouvères. Limousin marriage chest.

46 David as a shepherd, playing a harp; 12th century. This is a charming confusion of ideas, with the kingly instrument being played in a pastoral context.
Church of Saint-Gilles, Gard, France

47 King David playing the harp, with four tongued bells hanging above him; late 12th century. This harp has the slender forepillar and neck characteristic of the European or romanesque harp.
Westminster Psalter   *British Museum, London*

48 A figure representing Music, with psaltery, small fiddle with incurved sides, and bells. The figure below represents Mathematics.   *Chartres Cathedral*

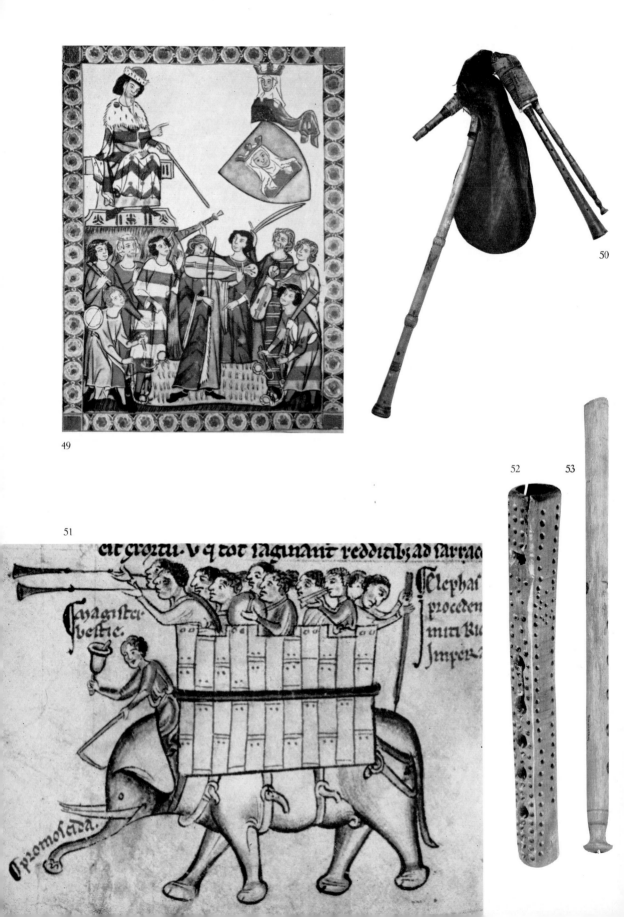

49

50

51

52 53

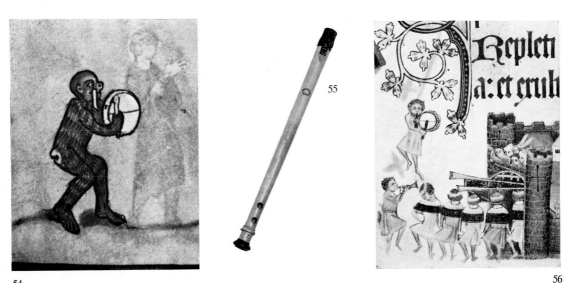

54

55

56

49 Heinrich von Meissen (generally called Frauenlob), founder of the first Mastersingers school, with a band of pupils; *c* 1300. The instruments, from left to right, are tabor, recorder, shawm whose conical bore and large fan-shaped reed are clearly shown, large and small five-stringed oval fiddles, pig's head psaltery held upside down, and bagpipe with single chanter and two drones, one in the same stock as the chanter.
University Library, Heidelberg

50 *Cornemuse* from Berry, France. This folk bagpipe is of the same type as that in plate 49, with chanter and short drone in the same stock and a separate long drone.
Pitt Rivers Museum, Oxford

51 A procession of welcome to Earl Richard of Cornwall at Cremona in 1241. Two trumpeters, a drummer and a player of double pipes are among a dozen figures on elephant-back. The *magister bestie* sounds a large hand-bell.
Chronicle of Matthew Paris
Corpus Christi College, Cambridge

52 A fipple flute of red deer bone, found at White Castle, Monmouth; second half of the 13th century. The fipple is missing. The external shape is square; the bore is roughly cylindrical.
National Museum of Wales, Cardiff

53 Wooden fipple flute from Kharkov. This folk example, with mouthpiece slightly shaped into a 'beak', is a stage nearer the familiar recorder than the bone instrument in plate 52.
Pitt Rivers Museum, Oxford

1300–1500

54 A monkey playing a pipe and tabor; *c* 1300. Although the pipe has only three holes – two for fingers and one for thumb – the player gets a complete scale by using harmonics.
British Museum, London

55 A modern Béarnais three-hole pipe, with the maker's mark *Prosper Colas à Paris* stamped on the front. This is still a popular and useful instrument in the southern French and Basque provinces, where it is played with a tabor or with a 'stringed drum' (see plate 97).
Pitt Rivers Museum, Oxford

56 A *carole* danced by men to the accompaniment of pipe and tabor and small shawm; early 14th century. Two long trumpets, whose players are out of sight, protrude through the city gate.
Luttrell Psalter
British Museum, London

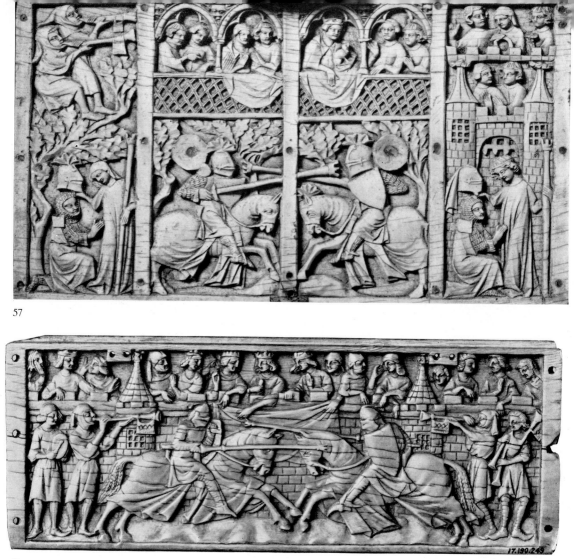

57

58

57 Two trumpeters at a joust; early 14th century. The
word 'trumpet', which has a precise contemporary
meaning, is also used indiscriminately for all medieval
trumpet-like instruments, including the high herald's
trumpet known as *clarion* and the long *buzine*.
Ivory Tabernacle   *National Museum, Ravenna*

58 A 14th-century joust, with attendant musicians
playing tabor and long trumpet (*buzine*) on the left, a
clarion and bagpipes with double chanter and single
drone on the right.
Ivory plaque; gift of J. Pierpoint Morgan, 1917
                        Metropolitan Museum of Art, New York

59 A saints' *carole* accompanied by the gittern, an early
type of guitar-like instrument
Queen Mary's Psalter   *British Museum, London*

60 An illustrated text of the *Roman de la rose* written in
England in the second half of the 14th century,
showing the *carole* danced to the music of treble and
alto shawm and bagpipe. The poem (most of which

was written in the previous century) spoke of 'fleu-
teurs et menestriers et jugleeurs' but the artist presumably illustrated the practice of his own time.
                                    Bodleian Library, Oxford

61 A 14th-century chess game, with background music on
a psaltery, played with quill plectra
Ivory comb   *Archives Photographiques, Paris*

62 *Exultate* initial with figures playing pipe and tabor,
finger-plucked psaltery, large fiddle and long trumpet,
with a singer; c 1325. This initial of Psalm 80 was frequently illustrated with musician figures. The assem-
blage of instruments is not necessarily to be taken as
representing those which played together.
Bromholm Psalter   *Bodleian Library, Oxford*

63 Positive organ of the early 14th century, of the kind
which was set on a choir-screen. Reversals of the correct order of pipes appear fairly frequently in medieval
depictions.
Peterborough Psalter   *Royal Library, Brussels*

59

61

62

64   64

65

66

64 Tranverse flute played by a fantastic figure; c 1320
Book of Hours of Jeanne d'Evreux
Metropolitan Museum of Art, New York
The Cloisters Collection, Purchase, 1954

65 Long drum beaten with light hooked sticks, recorder
and flat cymbals, in a detail from 'The Mocking of
Christ' fresco, painted by Mihajlo and Eutichije in
1317–18. Long drum and cymbals did not become
common in western Europe until the 18th century.
Church of St George, Staro Nagoricino, Serbia

66 Droneless bagpipe, hurdy-gurdy, shawm, portative
organ and small kettle-drums are crudely depicted in
this marginal illustration from *Le Roman d'Alexandre*,
done in 1344.   *Bodleian Library, Oxford*

67 The Angers Tapestry of the Apocalypse was made for
Louis, first Duke of Anjou. It was completed in 1380,
from design drawings made at least five years earlier.
The many musician figures woven into the border
include remarkably early depictions of certain instruments (*b, c, d, g* and *j*).

a Kettle-drums

b A shallow drum of the type now called a bass drum.
The heads are nailed to the body, not braced like
those on the Turkish long drum in plate 65.

c Flat cymbals, played with the up-and-down movement of the antique cup-shaped cymbals

67a

67b

67c

67d Triangle with jingles

 e Short trumpet, possibly meant to be a draw-trumpet

 f Long trumpet

 g Beaten 'bichord', or two-stringed drum (see plate 97)

 h Short-necked, three-stringed oval fiddle. The bow is still like a *lira* bow (see plate 41).

 j Cornett. A refined form of the simple animal horn with finger-holes, it was made of wood bound with leather, and had a separate, cup-shaped mouthpiece. It is not known to have been in common use until the 16th century.

67d

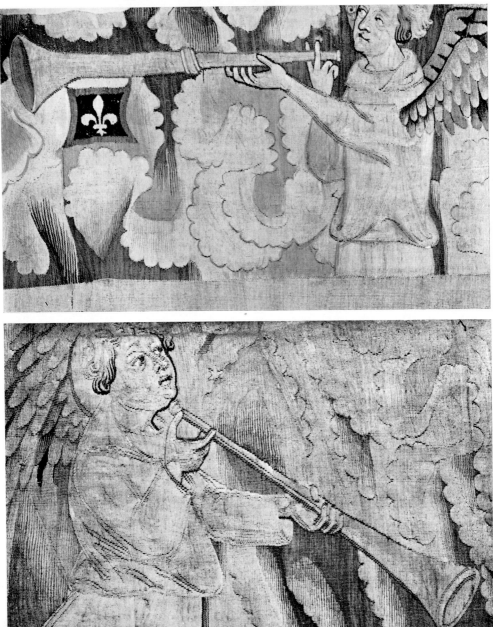

67e

67f

67g

67h

67j

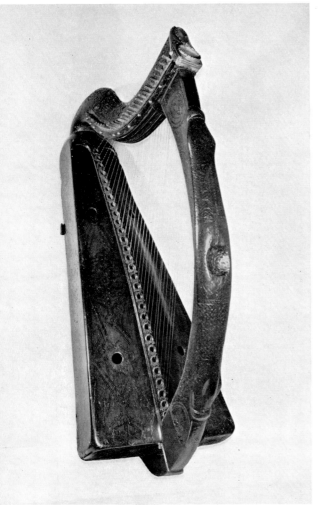

68 69

68 Harper and recorder-player carved on a misericord; 14th century *Chichester Cathedral, Sussex*

69 Recorder found under a 15th-century house in Dordrecht *Gemeentemuseum, The Hague*

70 Small Irish harp; 14th or 15th century. The Irish harp was an enormously strong and robust instrument, with a thick soundbox cut from one solid piece of willow, a heavy neck and a curved forepillar; its brass strings were plucked with long fingernails. The instrument's basic form varied remarkably little in its four centuries of recorded history *Trinity College, Dublin*

71 Charles V of France and the Emperor Charles IV at dinner in the Grand Palais in 1377. The French king's trumpeter has the straight clarion; the German trumpeter plays the S-shaped instrument. Chronicle of France *British Museum, London*

72 Mounted shawm- and clarion-players attendant on the Emperor Sigismond at the Council of Constance 1411–18. This important political and ecclesiastical congress, which ended the Great Schism, was attended in full pomp by princes of the Church and high clergy from all over Europe. Chronicle of Ulrich von Richental

73 Psaltery played with quill plectra; 1420. This is an exact depiction of the playing position. Stained glass from the Burgkirche, Lübeck *St-Annen-Museum, Lübeck*

74 Russian *gusle*, a folk instrument of the psaltery type, used for accompanying songs and laments, and for solo dance tunes. It sometimes appears in the instrumental ensembles of the big Russian song-and-dance companies, where its gentle sound is hardly audible among the lustier accordions and balalaikas. *Pitt Rivers Museum, Oxford*

70

71

72

73

74

75a

75b

76

75 The marble reliefs made in the 1430s by Luca dell[a] Robbia for the Cantoria (singers' gallery) of th[e] Cathedral of Florence contain generally realisti[c] instrumentalists and singers.
   a Straight and folded trumpets, and recorders carrie[d] by the three boys in the background
   b Three-hole pipe and tabors

Cathedral Museum, Florenc[e]

76 Positive organ, Renaissance harp and large five[-]stringed oval fiddle on the altarpiece painted by Ja[n] van Eyck and completed in 1432. The Renaissanc[e] harp, with a very shallow soundbox and almo[st] straight forepillar, had its strings fixed in the bo[dy] by right-angled wooden pegs which gave a jarrin[g] quality to the sound. The fiddle has a large body but comparatively short vibrating string length.

St Bavo, Ghe[nt]

77 Musician angels in the Beauchamp window, designe[d] by John Prudde; 1447. Above, left to right, are doub[le] hornpipe, single hornpipe, straight and curve[d] cornetts(?), the mouthpieces not clearly depicte[d] and double hornpipe again. Below are harpsichor[d] positive organ, clavichord, bagpipe and triangle.

St Mary's Church, Warwi[ck]

78 Welsh pibcorn or single hornpipe. Hornpipes, st[ill] found in Europe, north Africa and west Asia, surviv[ed] in Wales until the 18th century. The bore of the pi[pe] itself is cylindrical; it is sounded by a simple sing[le] reed, of the type shown on the little pipe in plate [?] but made as a separate unit. A horn is added to t[he] lower end of the pipe, and the reed is enclosed in [an] added mouth-horn.

Welsh Folk Museum, St Fagans, Car[diff]

77

78

82a

79 Organ in St Mary's Church, Lübeck; built in 1477, destroyed in 1942. From the mid-15th century onwards larger organs had two keyboards: a 'Great Organ' with a number of pipes answering to each key to give the unison, octave and higher harmonics, making a bright, clangorous 'chorus', and a '*Rückpositiv*' with generally a fipple flute solo 'stop' and a less powerful 'chorus' than on the Great. The English name 'Choir Organ' for the *Rückpositiv* is a misnomer for the French term '*chaire de l'orgue*', i.e., the positive originally at the organist's back, as it is in this organ.

Formerly in St Mary's, Lübeck

82b

80 Shawms and folded trumpet at a banquet; 1496. The association of shawms, or hoboys as they were later called in England, with feasting and hospitality was still current in Shakespeare's time.
'The Feast of Ahasuerus'   *St-Annen-Museum, Lübeck*

81 Detail from 'Acrobats and Wrestlers' by Apollonio di Giovanni (*d* 1463) showing musicians playing two small lutes during the display *Ashmolean Museum, Oxford*

82 *a* Musician angels in a fresco of the 'Calling of the Elect'; 1499–1504, restored in the present century. They play lutes of three different sizes, Renaissance harp, guitar, oval fiddle and tambourines. What may be a *lira da braccio* is being tuned.
b Detail of guitarist-angel who is singing to her own accompaniment   *Orvieto Cathedral*

83 Three Renaissance harps, three large recorders and three Renaissance mandoras, played by angels in a detail from 'The Crowning of the Virgin', by the Master of the life of Mary (1465–90)
Alte Pinakothek, Munich

83

84

85

86

84 Angel musician with a rebec, in 'Madonna with Angels' by Cosimo Roselli (1439–1507). The rebec was three-stringed and pear-backed like the earlier *lira*, but, unlike its medieval predecessors, also had a separate, raised fingerboard. It seems to have been used chiefly for dance music. *Uffizi Gallery, Florence*

85 A musician tuning a *lira da braccio*, by Cosimo Tura (c 1430–95). Four strings lie over the fingerboard, a single bourdon string lies to the side. The fine construction, with ebony fingerboard and purfling round the edge of the body, is clearly visible. The bow has a shaped stick (compare with that in plate 67*h*). *National Gallery of Ireland, Dublin*

86 Angel playing a small fretted five-stringed fiddle, from the St Ursula shrine by Hans Memling (1433–94) *St John's Hospital, Bruges*

87 'A Concert' by Lorenzo Costa (c 1460–1535). The lute
accompanying the three singers is the large lute, light
and fragile in construction, small but expressive in
sound, which became standard throughout the next
century. A recorder with gently cut-away mouthpiece, and a small fretted fiddle whose primitive bow
construction is clearly visible, lie on the table.

National Gallery, London

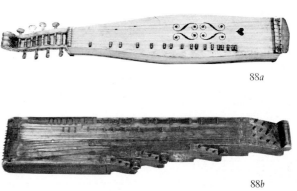

88a

88 At some time in the late Middle Ages frets were
applied to folk instruments of the zither or psaltery
type. The Norwegian *langeleik* (a) has frets under one
string, and seven open strings which give a thrummed
drone accompaniment to the tune on the fretted
melody string. The Hungarian *tambura* (b) is a more
complex instrument, with double or triple stringing
throughout, and three sets of short drone strings as
well as the long ones. *Pitt Rivers Museum, Oxford*

88b

89*a*

89*b*

89 'The Triumphs of Maximilian' – illustrations to a chronicle of the great deeds of the Emperor – were the outcome of many years' work by several artists, some of whose designs were rejected as too old-fashioned and medieval for the new humanist grandeur of the Emperor. Maximilian approved the final plan only a year before his death in 1519, and Hans Burgkmair's magnificent woodcuts appeared in 1526. The processions include several waggons carrying musicians.

a Mounted trumpeters and kettle-drummers

b Chamber organ played by Paul Hofhaimer, Maximilian's blind court organist

c Wind ensemble of two cromornes, two shawms and sackbut

d Three lute players and two viol players

89c

89d

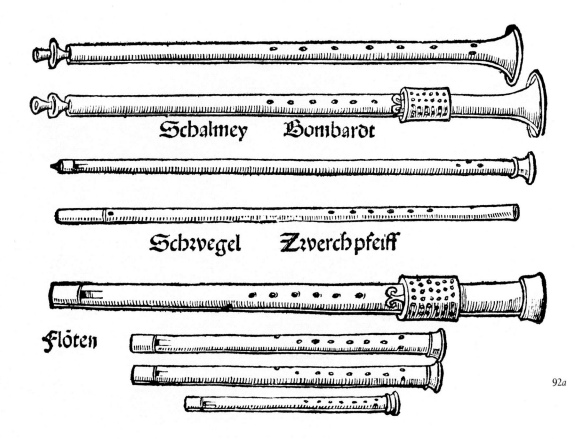

Schalmey   Bombardt

Schwegel   Zwerchpfeiff

Flöten

92a

90 A flute quartet by Urs Graf (1485–1527). These flutes, of plain cylindrical bore, must have had a strong, solid sound, as effective in the open air as indoors.

Kunstmuseum, Basel

91 Title page of Silvestro di Ganassi's *Fontegara*, 1535, showing a recorder consort and two singers performing from part books. Three viols and a lute hang on the wall behind and a cornett and cornettino are in the foreground.

92 Sebastian Virdung's *Musica getutscht* of 1511 was the first

vernacular textbook on musical instruments. Besides giving illustrations and descriptions of most current instruments, it gave methods of adapting vocal music to the organ, lute and flute.

a Treble shawm (*Schalmey*), tenor shawm (*Bombardt*), three-hole fipple flute (*Schwegel*), transverse flute (*Zwerchpfeiff*) and four recorders (*Flöten*). The 'pirouette' – a socket into which the reed was fitted and against which the shawmist supported his lips, as the Oriental shawmist does against a flat disk – can be seen clearly in Virdung's illustration.

Sackpfeiff

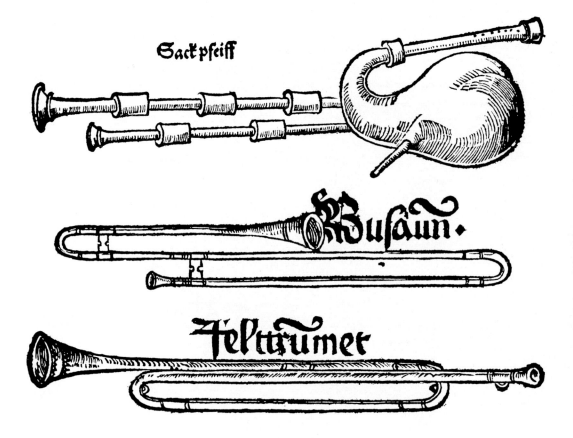

Busaun.

Feltrumet

Clareta

Thurner horn

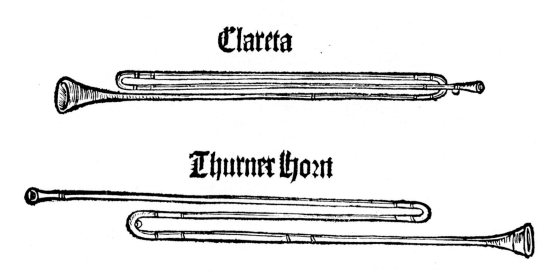

92b

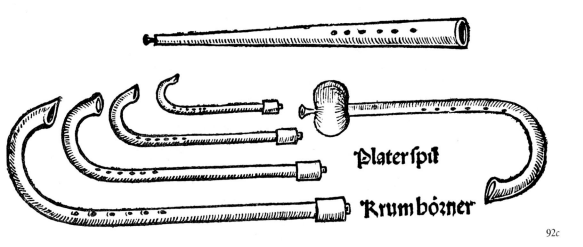

Platerspil

Krumhörner

92c

92d

Lyra

92e

2 *b* Bagpipe (*Sackpfeiff*), trombone (*Busaūn*), field trumpet (*Felttruūmet*), clarin trumpet (*Clareta*) and the last
  survivor of the old S-shaped trumpet (*Thurnerhorn*)

c Straight cornett, bladder-pipe (*Platerspil*) and four
  cromornes (*Krumhörner*)

d Rustic and hunting instruments – beaten pot,
  bells, coiled and curved hunting horns, clappers
  and Jew's harp

e Hurdy-gurdy (*Lyra*)

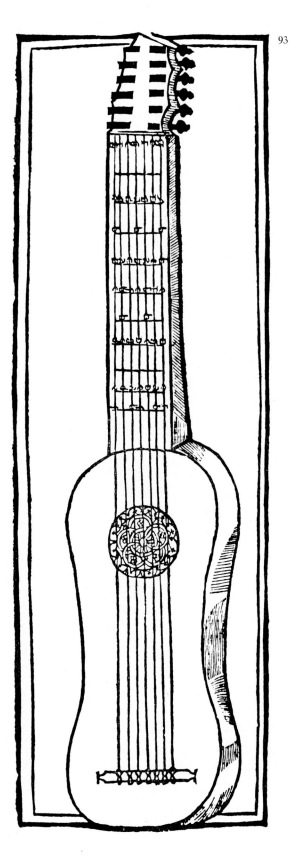

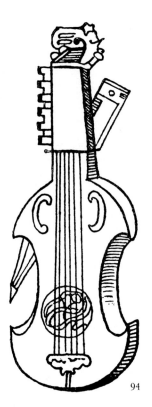

94

93 *Vihuela* illustrated diagrammatically in Juan Bermudo's *Declaración de Instrumentos Musicales* of 1555. Tuned like a lute but resembling a shallow guitar in form, it was the courtly instrument of 16th-century Spain.

94 Martin Agricola's *Musica Instrumentalis Deutsch*, published in 1528, is a vulgarized version of Virdung's book. Though inaccurate in many respects, it gives a few instruments not illustrated by Virdung, such as this keyed fiddle (*Schlüssel fidel*), which had keyed string-stoppers like the hurdy-gurdy but was sounded with a hand-operated bow.

95 Two woodcuts from Hans Holbein's 'Dance of Death' series; 1523–5. On the left is Death playing a xylophone – the first known depiction of this instrument; on the right are hurdy-gurdy, two cromornes, trumpets and kettle-drums.

96 Sixteenth-century German dulcimer, or hammered psaltery. The use of hammers or beaters instead of plectra seems to have started at the end of the 15th century. In its large forms (Greek *santouri* and Hungarian *cimbalon*) it is a bright and lively component in eastern European popular bands.   *Pitt Rivers Museum, Oxford*

97 Béarnais strung drum and three-hole pipe. This is the dulcimer reduced to its simplest terms – six strings tuned to tonic and dominant throughout, beaten to provide a rhythmic bass to the tune on the pipe.
Pitt Rivers Museum, Oxford

95

96

97

98 Bass viol, chamber organ, flute, *lira da braccio* and
spitzharfe (upright double psaltery) in 'Musical Ladies'
by Tintoretto (1518–94)   *Pinakothek, Dresden*

99

An accurate depiction of the solid, one-piece recorder
of the 16th century, in a realistic portrait of a girl by
Giovanni Girolamo Savoldo (1480–1548)

Conte Alessandro Contini-Bonacorsi, Florence

100 Harpsichord by Jerome of Bologna; 1521. This, the earliest in date of all surviving harpsichords, is a sizeable instrument, over six feet long. Harpsichords of this size were presumably made to play with large ensembles. Although this instrument has two sets of strings of the same pitch, there is no means of 'stopping' the jacks of one set in order to get a change of dynamic level. Harpsichords with stops (mechanism to take out or combine two or three sets of strings, or to apply plectra of various materials) have survived only from later in the century. The principle had, however, been used on the organ for a century and it may have been applied early to the large harpsichord.

Victoria and Albert Museum, London (Crown copyright)

100

101

101 Sixteenth-century Italian clavichord. With its expressive but tiny sound, the clavichord was essentially a domestic instrument, which could delight the player and close-at-hand listeners.
Museum of the Conservatoire, Paris

102 'Girl Playing a Clavichord' by Jan van Hemessen; 1534
Worcester Art Museum, Massachusetts, U.S.A.

103 An ensemble of singer, large lute and bass viol in a detail from the 'Finding of Moses' by Bonifazio Veronese (1487–1553). This is a curious combination for the mid-16th century; the earlier use of instruments and voices playing parts in a *chanson* or *frottola* was outmoded, and the 17th-century chordal style of tune plus bass plus filling-in instrument had not yet fully evolved. *Ashmolean Museum, Oxford*

102

103

104 A raid on a village, the marauders led by a bagpiper whose instrument has one chanter and two drones; from Derricke's *Image of Ireland*, 1581. The native Irish use of bagpipes as martial and ceremonial instruments was remarked on by Vincenzo Galilei, lutenist and composer, and father of the astronomer.

105 Figures from Arbeau's *Orchésographie*; 1588. This book gave a detailed account of the steps and music of the fashionable dances of the 16th century, and of infantry marching routines and their accompanying music.

a Three-hole pipe and drum

b Hoboy (from French *hautbois*). This was the later 16th- and 17th-century name for the shawm. Arbeau said: 'Nowadays there is no workman so humble that he does not wish to have hoboys and sackbuts at his wedding.'

c Small recorder (*arigot*), side drum, flute, with two pikemen in formation. Below is a sample of the 'syllabization' of a simple drum rhythm.

105*a*

105*b*

105*c*

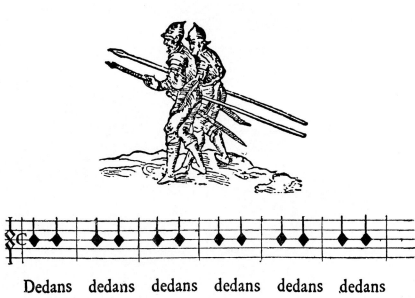

Dedans   dedans   dedans   dedans   dedans   dedans

106

107

108a

106 Italian virginal, 16th century, which bears the arms of Queen Elizabeth I and almost certainly belonged to her. Virginal was the usual English term for a small harpsichord with strings running roughly parallel to the keyboard, the bass strings being at the front. It is sometimes used more specifically for those with rectangular outer cases, those in polygonal cases being called spinets.
   Victoria and Albert Museum, London (Crown copyright)

107 Combined harpsichord and organ made in London in 1579 by the Flemish maker, Ludovic Theeuwes. Instruments of this kind, with organ and harpsichord sounding together, were not uncommon in the 16th century; some had more than one register on each instrument and must therefore have had a considerable range of tonal possibilities.
   Victoria and Albert Museum, London (Crown copyright)

108 *a* Violin (1564) and *b* viola (1574) made by Andrea Amati.
   Ashmolean Museum, Oxford

108b

110

Lira da braccio, 1540, by Giovanni Maria da Brescia. It has five fingered strings and two bourdon strings off the fingerboard.   *Ashmolean Museum, Oxford*

Lyra-viol, 1598, by John Rose. This non-consort, chord-playing viol was intermediate in size between the tenor and bass viols. It was tuned 'lyra-way', in alternate fourths and fifths after the manner of the new freakish bass of the *lira da braccio* which was called *lira da gamba* or *lirone*.   *Ashmolean Museum, Oxford*

Seventeenth-century Italian cittern
                              Ashmolean Museum, Oxford

111

113

Scenes from the life of Sir Henry Unton in a mural by an unknown painter; 1597. On the left a viol consort accompanies a little singing boy. A masked procession goes with torches to the sound of a side drum. In the foreground a broken consort of violin, flute, bandora, cittern, bass viol and lute is playing.

National Portrait Gallery, London

113 Violin, lute and cornett in a musical group painted by Bartolomeo Manfredi (1580–1620). The playing positions of the violin and lute are shown fairly correctly – the former in the then usual on-the-chest position. The cornettist's left hand is too far down the instrument, leaving two finger-holes uncoverable.

Uffizi Gallery, Florence

114 Music by a choir and cornetts and sackbuts, during Mass celebrated by a bishop; *Ecomium Musices*, 1590

1610–1750

115 Combined two-manual harpsichord and virginal, 1619, by Ruckers. Instruments made by the Ruckers family of Antwerp were highly regarded in the 17th and 18th centuries. Most surviving examples were altered and enlarged during the 18th century. One Ruckers harpsichord (in the Germanisches Museum, Nuremberg) has been restored to its original state.
Museum of the Conservatoire, Brussels

116 Spinet lid, painted in 1619 by Friedrich von Falckenberg, showing a consort of violin, viola, tenor and bass viols and organ-cum-virginal. As the virginal (or spinet) is a separate instrument from the organ, the two could be played in separate parts, as appears to be the case here. *Germanisches Museum, Nuremberg*

115

116

117

118

117 Bass viol with cello-shaped body, alternatively six-stringed cello, by the brothers Amati; 1611. The form and size of violin and viol family instruments were not standardized at this time. *Ashmolean Museum, Oxford*

118 Tenor viol by Ernest Busch (the frets are missing); 1617
Museum of Music History, Copenhagen

119 Tambourine and large violin held in 'Musicians and Soldiers' by Valentin (1580–1620). *Art Gallery, Strasbourg*

120 Two double-course guitars and a small violin in 'A Musical Trio' by Velasquez; 1619. Double courses (two strings tuned in unison or at the octave) were usual on 17th-century guitars.

Art Gallery, Berlin-Dahlem

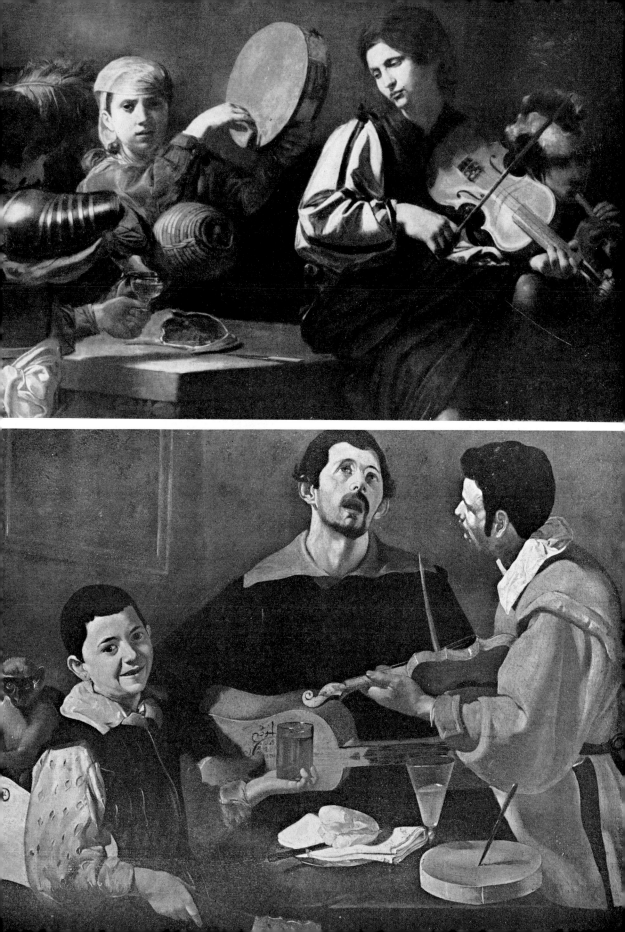

121 Double-course guitar and lute in 'Spanish Students' by
Theodoor Rombouts (1597–1637). The double-course
guitar, with the now standard six courses, is familiar
today chiefly from its use by American folk-singers
such as Huddie Ledbetter and Pete Seeger.

Alte Pinakothek, Munich

122 The *Syntagma* of Michael Praetorius published between
1615 and 1620 was an encyclopaedic work on music.
The section on instruments contains valuable scale
drawings and accounts of current instrumental
practice.

a Art and popular stringed instruments
1 and 2 Rebec and kit 'an octave higher'
3 Small violin 'a fourth higher'
4 Violin
5 Viola
6 Five-stringed cello
7 Four-stringed *tromba marina*. This freakish instrument
with one melody string on which only harmonics
were played and one or more drone strings appeared
in the 15th century and enjoyed a limited vogue
until the 18th. Its origins are obscure.
8 Fretted zither

XXI

1. 2. Kleine Poschen / Geigen ein Octav höher. 3. Discant-Geig ein Quart höher.
4. Rechte Discant-Geig. 5. Tenor-Geig. 6 Bas-Geig de bracio. 7. Trumscheidt.
8. Scheidtholtt.

12

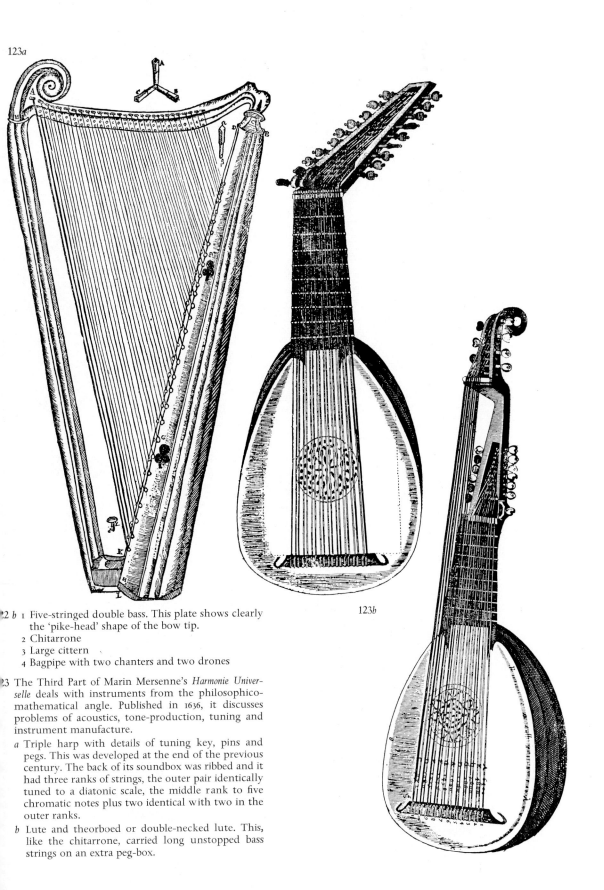

123a

123b

2 *b* 1 Five-stringed double bass. This plate shows clearly
the 'pike-head' shape of the bow tip.
2 Chitarrone
3 Large cittern
4 Bagpipe with two chanters and two drones

23 The Third Part of Marin Mersenne's *Harmonie Univer-
selle* deals with instruments from the philosophico-
mathematical angle. Published in 1636, it discusses
problems of acoustics, tone-production, tuning and
instrument manufacture.

a Triple harp with details of tuning key, pins and
pegs. This was developed at the end of the previous
century. The back of its soundbox was ribbed and it
had three ranks of strings, the outer pair identically
tuned to a diatonic scale, the middle rank to five
chromatic notes plus two identical with two in the
outer ranks.

b Lute and theorboed or double-necked lute. This,
like the chitarrone, carried long unstopped bass
strings on an extra peg-box.

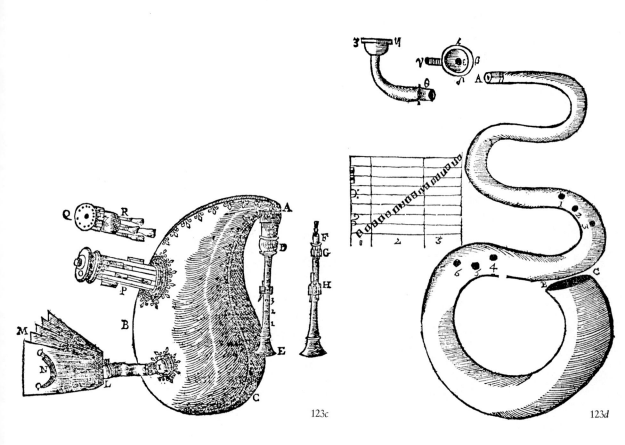

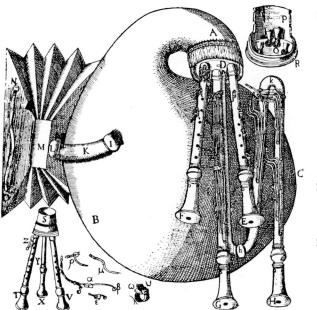

123c

123d

123e

123 c *Musette*, or small bellows-blown French chamber bagpipe. Details of chanter and drones are shown beside the complete instrument.

   d Serpent, with details of mouthpiece, and range. Originally an improved form of large cornett, this was said by Mersenne to be a useful substitute or reinforcement for low voices 'as singers with low bass voices are very rare'.

   e *Sourdeline*, or Italian chamber bagpipe, with four melody pipes. No other wind instrument of this period had such complicated keywork. The small diagram on the left shows the pipes of a smaller instrument.

124 French *musette*, late 17th or 18th century, with six-keyed main chanter (*grand chalumeau*), and auxiliary chanter (*petit chalumeau*) of the type added by Jean Hotteterre   *Pitt Rivers Museum, Oxford*

125 A figure of Polyphemus playing a *sourdeline*; 17th century, Italian. This has the long goatskin bag which Mersenne represented inaccurately by one like that in the French *musette*.

Crosby Brown Collection of Musical Instruments, 1889
Metropolitan Museum of Art, New York

24

25

126

127

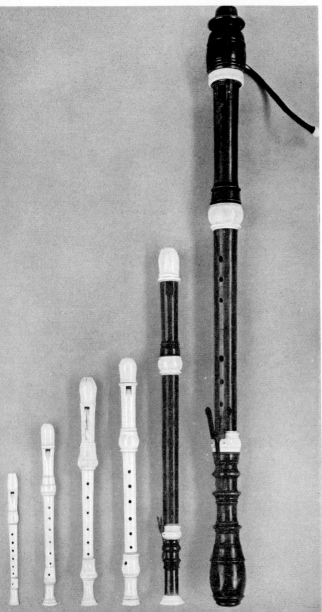

126 Spinet lid showing Italian rustic music; 17th century. The instruments are a *tricche-ballache* (folk rhythm-instrument consisting of several loose hammers in a frame, which beat against a fixed central hammer), a shawm, a *colascione* (long-necked three-stringed lute of Middle Eastern type, popular in 17th-century Italy) and a large tambourine. *Deutsches Museum, Munich*

127 Six recorders of the new narrow-bored jointed type. The three instruments at the right were made by Jean Hotteterre (instrument maker to Louis XIV), who, with some of his colleagues, transformed wood-wind design in the middle of the 17th century.
Museum of the Conservatoire, Paris;
third from right, collection G. Thibault, on deposit

128 One-keyed flute by Gerock of London. The one-keyed flute was used until the end of the 18th century; this is a late example. *Joan Rimmer*

129 Three-keyed oboe of early type by W. Kress, oboe d'amore by Dotzell and two tenor oboes by Lindner. (No reeds are shown, and the crooks of the tenor oboes are absent.) *Bavarian National Museum, Munich*

130 Wind ensemble of two oboes, tenor oboe and bassoon on the bell of an oboe by Beukers; late 17th century
Victoria and Albert Museum, London (Crown copyright)

128

129

130

131

131 *Les Douze Grands Hautbois Du Roi*, the Royal wind band of oboes, tenor oboes and bassoons, at the coronation of Louis XV in 1715

132 Great bass shawm, bought for the Marienkirche, Lübeck, in 1685, when Buxtehude was organist. German wind usage was conservative; the new bass instrument was the more expressive (and portable) bassoon, which is shown here beside the shawm.

St-Annen-Museum, Lübeck

133

134

133 Organ of Adlington Hall, near Macclesfield, Cheshire, built in the last quarter of the 17th century by Bernard Smith, restored in 1959 by Noel Mander. Bernhard Schmidt came from Halle to England in 1660 and built organs in Westminster Abbey, St Paul's and many other cathedrals and churches. The Adlington Hall organ is much the largest 17th-century organ in England, and is in the nearest condition to the original of any. The Great Organ has ten stops, including a full chorus up to the triple octave, a trumpet and a Vox Humana (a reed stop with short capped pipes); the Choir Organ has a flute and a bassoon. Though pedals had been on large organs on the continent since the second half of the 15th century, few English organs had them before the 19th century.

134 The Kildare harp; 17th century. This is a fine example of the large Irish harp which was developed during the late 16th century. Its thick and heavy soundbox increased in depth from bass to treble, giving greater

resonance to the treble strings than was possible in the earlier Irish harps, whose boxes were of the same depth all through.   *National Museum of Ireland, Dublin*

135 Triple-coiled horn by William Bull of London; 1699. Bull was one of the Royal trumpeters, and also a maker of trumpets and French horns.

Horniman Museum, London

136 Pianoforte by Bartolommeo Cristofori of Florence; 1720. It is inscribed *Bartholomaeus de Christophoris Patavinus Inventor Faciebat Florentiae MDCCXX*. The piano is a mechanized dulcimer with hammered strings, while the harpsichord is a mechanized psaltery with plucked strings. It is possible that the idea of a pianoforte, which, as its name implies, could play loudly or softly according to the player's touch, was suggested by the brilliant and effective musical results achieved on large dulcimers by popular virtuosi.

Crosby Brown Collection of Musical Instruments, 1889
Metropolitan Museum of Art, New York

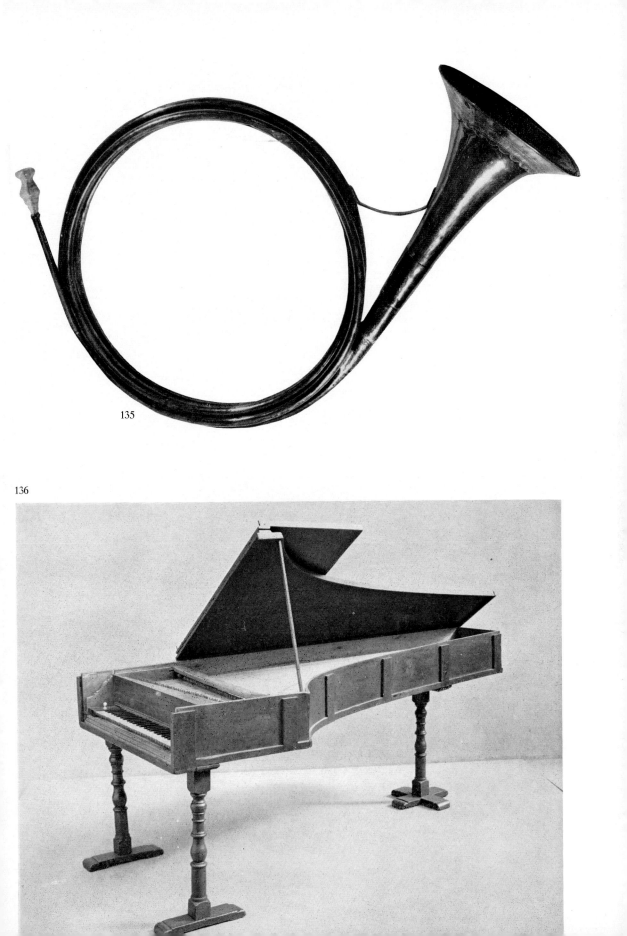

135

136

137 A page from *A Collection of the most Celebrated English and Scots Songs*, published in 1739. Song tune and figured bass (which accomplished amateurs as well as professionals were able to deal with) appear in the keyboard part. The tune is also given for the flute, which was then becoming the most popular wind instrument among amateurs.

138 Spinet by John Harrison; London 1749. Small polygonal harpsichords of this kind were the usual domestic keyboard instruments in the first part of the 18th century.

Taphouse Collection, on loan to the Faculty of Music, Oxford

137

138

139

140

139 High-headed triple harp, by David Evans; London
   1736. By this time, both triple harps and Irish harps
   were made with high pointed fronts which gave extra
   length to the bass strings.
      Victoria and Albert Museum, London (Crown copyright)

140 Nansi Richards Jones, only surviving player trained on
   the triple harp. Wales was the only place where the
   triple harp survived to any extent beyond the mid-
   18th century. Mrs Richards Jones learnt both technique
   and repertoire from gipsies and rural players, who
   retained baroque techniques to some degree.

141 Bavarian hooked harp; early 18th century. The large
   hooks fitted in the neck beside certain strings were
   turned by hand to shorten those strings and so raise
   their pitch by a semitone. This clumsy method of
   pitch changing was the starting point in the evolution
   of the mechanized pedal harp.
      Crosby Brown Collection of Musical Instruments, 1889
      Metropolitan Museum of Art, New York   141

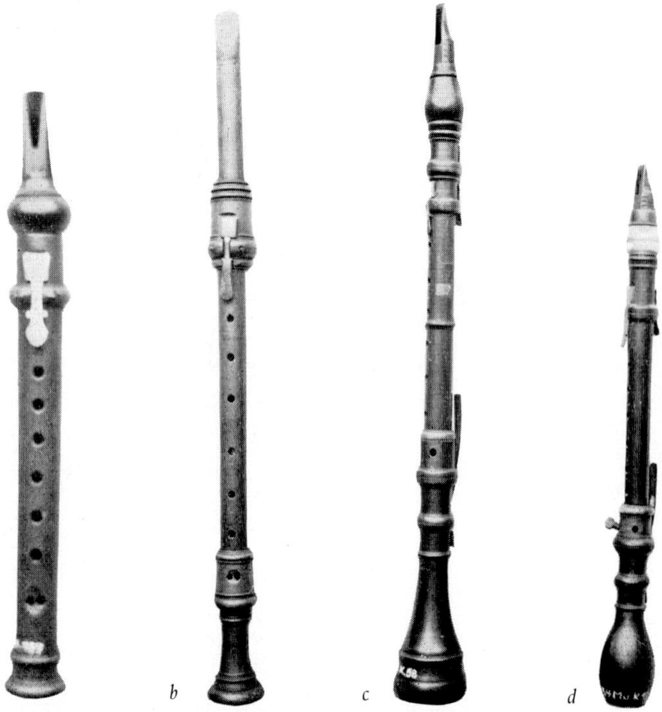

142 *a* *b* *c* *d*

39

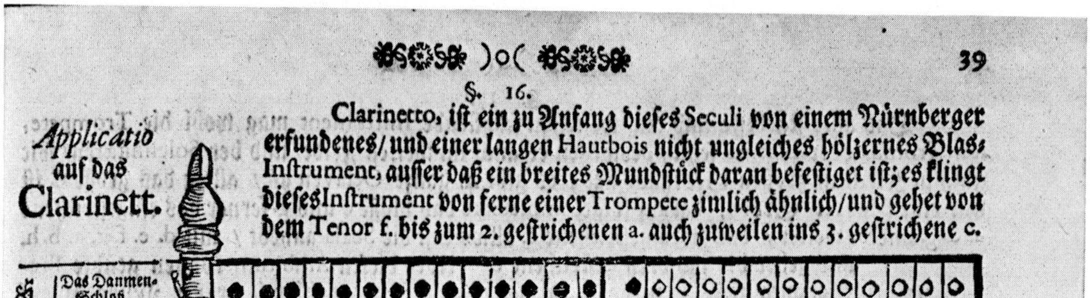

§. 16.

Applicatio auf das Clarinett.

Clarinetto, ist ein zu Anfang dieses Seculi von einem Nürnberger erfundenes/ und einer langen Hautbois nicht ungleiches hölzernes Blas-Instrument, ausser daß ein breites Mundstück daran befestiget ist; es klingt dieses Instrument von ferne einer Trompete zimlich ähnlich/ und gehet von dem Tenor f. bis zum 2. gestrichenen a. auch zuweilen ins 3. gestrichene c.

Linker Hand.
Das Daumen-Schloß.
Daumen-Loch.
Zeig-Finger. Schloß.
Loch.
Mittel-Finger.
Gold-Finger.
Rechter Hand
Zeig-Finger.
Mittel-Finger
Gold-Finger.
Klein Finger.
Systema Musicum samt den Noten.
f g gis a b h c cis d dis e f fis g a b h c cis d dis e f fis g gis a

Das

14

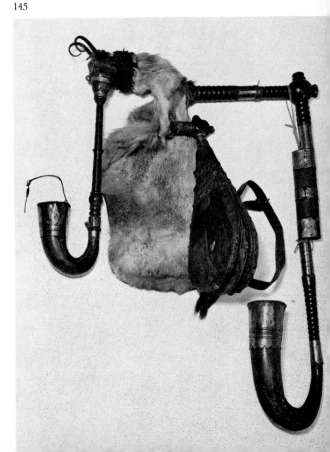

144

145

42 *a* Two-keyed chalumeau by Stuehnwal

   b Two-keyed clarinet in D (marked with the number
     1) by J. C. Denner

   c Three-keyed clarinet in G by J. W. Königsperger

   d Three-keyed clarinet in high G, maker unknown

All are shown without reeds; *a* is somewhat enlarged
in relation to the others, and *c* and *d* are shown in
profile. Denner's instrument shown here is a very
early model, if not his first.
Bavarian National Museum, Munich

43 Page from Joseph Majer's *Museum Musicum* of 1732,
showing a two-keyed clarinet and fingering chart.
The chart is incorrect for several notes, perhaps
because Majer was not himself familiar with the
instrument which was not yet in general use.

44 Balkan 'double-clarinet'. This double pipe is fitted
with single reeds of clarinet type, set on the front of
the mouthpiece, as is that in Majer's illustration. It is
impossible to tell whether folk instruments of this
kind preceded or followed the invention of the keyed
clarinet. *Gemeentemuseum, The Hague*

45 Bohemian bagpipe; 18th century. Both chanter and
drone are cylindrical in bore, though the former has
a conical exterior. Bagpipes of this kind have a particularly rich, burbling clarinetty sound.
Pitt Rivers Museum, Oxford

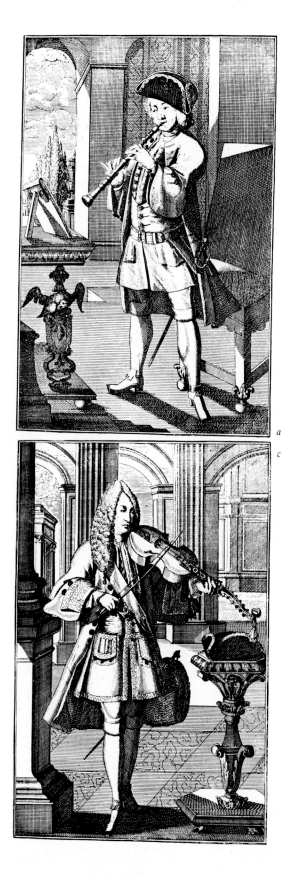

a

b

c

146

146 Three figures from Johann Christoph Weigel's
Musicalisches Theatrum, a set of engravings of instrumentalists made before 1740

  a Two-keyed clarinet

  b Double-coiled French horn. Although the name
  French horn was already applied to this instrument
  in the late 17th century, its use in indoor music
  seems to have been developed first in Germany.

  c *Viola d'amore*. In the 17th century, this name had been
  applied to a wire-strung violin. The *viola d'amore* of
  the mid-18th century was roughly the size of a viola,
  with six bowed strings of gut and a set of sympathetic wire strings. It also existed in violin size.

147 Hardanger fiddle, a Norwegian folk fiddle with four
bowed and four sympathetic strings, maybe a survivor
of the early, small form of *viola d'amore*, for it is traceable
from roughly the same date.

148 *Trompes de chasse* of the French *Chasseurs Alpins*. These are
survivals of the slender, double-coiled 18th-century
French horns.

156

151 Violin by George Perry of Dublin; 1741. This has been refitted with the tilted neck, longer fingerboard and higher bridge which became standard after 1800, when concert-giving circumstances and tastes in performance demanded bigger violin tone. Most old violins have been re-necked and very few remain in their original condition. *National Museum of Ireland, Dublin*

152 'Still Life With Violin and Recorder' by Jean-Baptiste Oudry; 1741. This shows clearly the short fingerboard, straight neck and sturdy bridge characteristic of violins made before the end of the 18th century. *Collection Cailleux, Paris*

150

149 Maracas, depicted in Filippo Bonanni's *Gabinetto Armonico* of 1722. This was a comprehensive, though sometimes inaccurate, book on instruments, lavishly illustrated. Bonanni was the first European author to deal fairly extensively with folk and extra-European instruments.

150 Baryton, by Norbert Bedler of Würtzburg; 1723. This was a bass instrument similar to the viola d'amore. It had no professional existence; the large number of pieces written for the baryton by Haydn were for private performance by his patron, Prince Nicholas Esterhazy, who was a devoted player. *Museum of the Conservatoire, Paris*

149

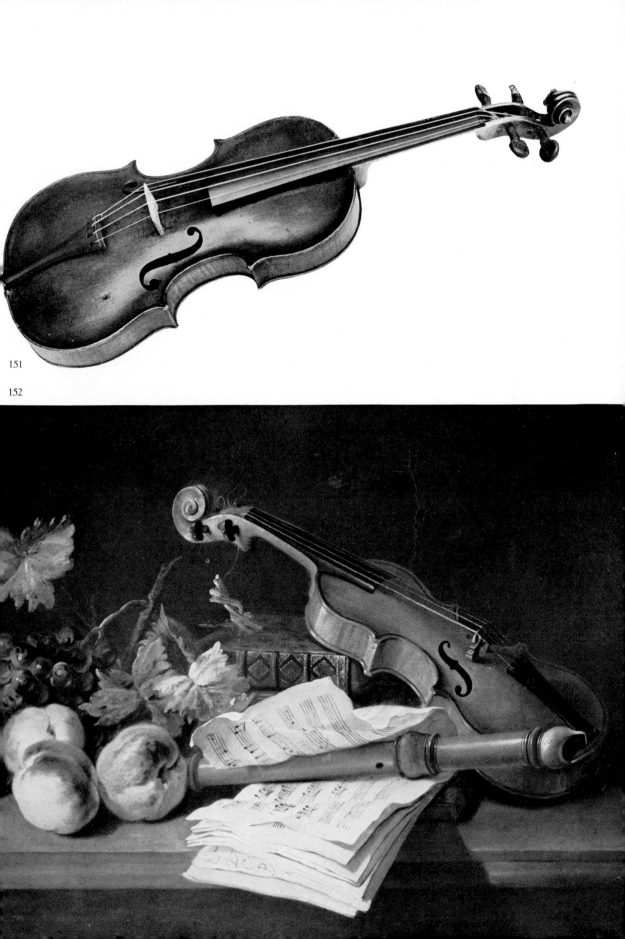

151

152

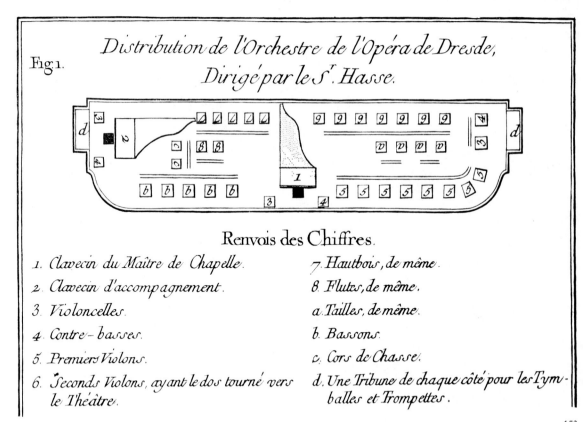

Fig. 1.

Distribution de l'Orchestre de l'Opéra de Dresde,
Dirigé par le S^r. Hasse.

Renvois des Chiffres.

1. Clavecin du Maître de Chapelle.
2. Clavecin d'accompagnement.
3. Violoncelles.
4. Contre-basses.
5. Premiers Violons.
6. Seconds Violons, ayant le dos tourné vers le Théâtre.

7. Hautbois, de même.
8. Flutes, de même.
a. Tailles, de même.
b. Bassons.
c. Cors de Chasse.
d. Une Tribune de chaque côté pour les Tymballes et Trompettes.

153

153 Plan of the orchestra at the Dresden Opera under Hasse, 1734–64

   1 Director's harpsichord
   2 Accompanying harpsichord
   3 Cellos
   4 Double basses
   5 First violins
   6 Second violins, their backs towards the stage
   7 Oboes, placed the same way
   8 Flutes, placed the same way
   a Violas, placed the same way
   b Bassoons
   c Horns
   d A balcony at each side for kettle-drums and trumpets

1750–1820

154 'Le Concert Champêtre' by François Drouais (1727–75) showing a group of French aristocratic amateurs with musette, one-keyed flute and violin

155 A hurdy-gurdy (*vielle à roue*) played by a French lady of fashion; 18th century. The playing of rustic instruments such as this was part of the mid-18th-century French craze for imitating pastoral life.

156 French hurdy-gurdy player from Berry; his instrument is identical with that in the previous plate.

154

155

156

157a

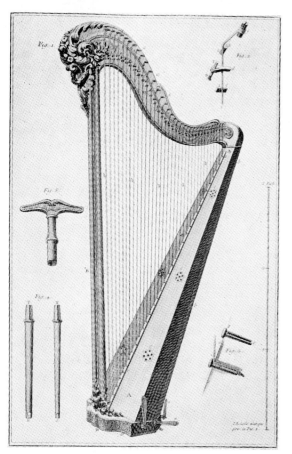

157b

157 The *Encyclopédie* of Diderot and D'Alembert, issued in Paris from 1751 onwards, was a vast illustrated work covering all aspects of knowledge and activity. Crafts, including the making of musical instruments, were dealt with in detail.

a An imaginary workshop. Four craftsmen are at work: one on an almost complete violin, one painting the forepillar of a harp, another boring pin-holes in a harp neck, the fourth planing a viola back. A hurdy-gurdy, a completed pedal harp, a harp soundbox, two bassoons and a cello stand on the floor. A cello body in clamps is on the bench. Violins and violas, a lute, a *colascione*, a guitar, a trumpet, a serpent and a bassoon are hanging on the wall. A dulcimer sits on a shelf with a row of organ pipes.

b Single-action pedal harp, with details of pins, tuning key, hook mechanism and pegs. The hooks were activated by mechanism inside the forepillar and neck, which was worked by pedals set in the base of the harp. Where the hooks turned by hand had only shortened one string, the mechanism attached to each pedal worked the strings of the same pitch name in every octave. Several harp makers are known to have been experimenting in the early 18th century with pedal mechanism. Credit for its invention is generally given to the Bavarian, Hochbrucker, who produced a pedal harp in 1720.

c Details of oboe construction, showing assembled instrument, silhouette of bore, separate joints, and reed, the last somewhat out of scale

d Details of flute and bass flute, showing complete instruments and separate joints. The head joint of the large flute is curved to minimize its holding length.

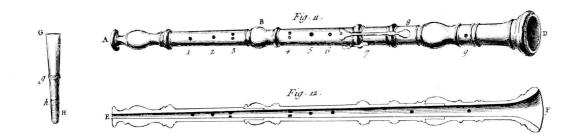

Fig. 11.

Fig. 12.

Fig. 13.   Fig. 14.   Fig. 15.

157c

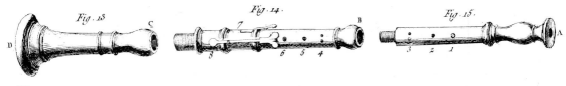

Fig. 28.

Fig. 29.

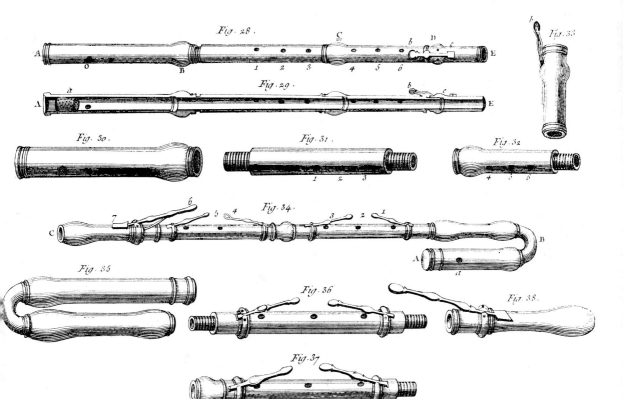

Fig. 30.   Fig. 31.   Fig. 32.

Fig. 34.

Fig. 35

Fig. 36.   Fig. 38.

Fig. 37.

157d

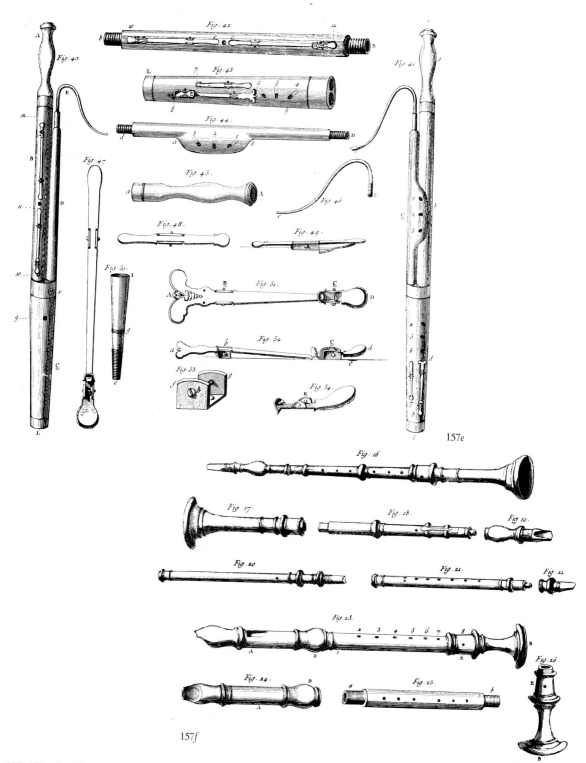

157e

157f

157 e Details of bassoon, showing both sides of a complete
instrument, separate joints with outlines of the
diagonally bored finger-holes, crook, key-fixing
mechanism, keys and reed – the three last out of
scale

  f Details of two-keyed clarinet, keyless chalumeau
and recorder, not in scale with each other. The

clarinet is inaccurately given a slightly conical
exterior, but is correct in other respects.

158 Church, formerly Abbey, of Amorbach, in the Oden-
wald, Bavaria, built 1742–7, with organ built by the
brothers Stumm, 1774–82. The organ case in baroque
and rococo churches is an integral part of their visual
effect.   *Abbey Church, Amorbach*

159

160

159 'The Minuet' by John Zoffany (c 1734–1810) shows a one-keyed flute and a small square (actually oblong) piano. These delicate pianos must have found great favour with amateurs from the middle of the 18th century, long before there was any characteristic piano music.

160 Six-keyed flute by Henry Potter; London 1777. The flute, as the least chromatically efficient of the 18th-century woodwind, was the first to be given keys to get good chromatic notes. Several London makers experimented in the 1760s with four keys, and six-keyed flutes were common by the end of the century.
Horniman Museum, London

161 Detail of a five-octave clavichord by Gottfried Joseph Horn; Nickern 1790. The large clavichord was still a usual family instrument in Germany when the square piano was becoming increasingly popular elsewhere.
Deutsches Museum, Munich

162 Detail of a square piano by Zumpe and Buntebart; London 1777. The jack which strikes the hammer when the key is depressed is visible on the detached key. The hand stops at the left (introduced by Zumpe) operate mechanisms which mute all the strings or lift the dampers from either treble or bass strings.
F. Ll. Harrison

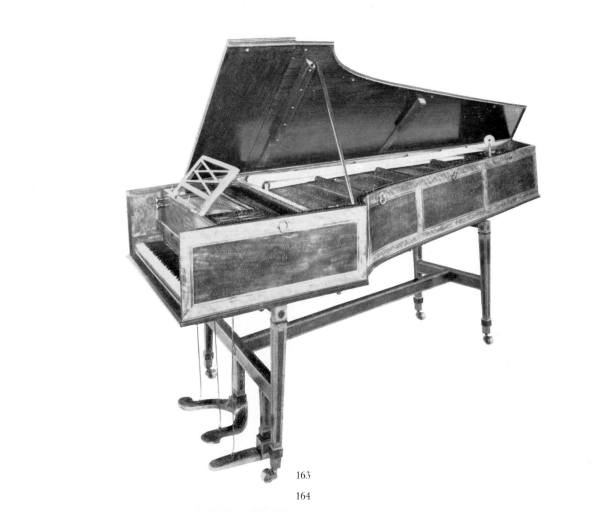

163

164

163 Combined harpsichord and pianoforte by Joseph Merlin; London 1789. The harpsichord has three sets of strings and three rows of jacks. The pianoforte has one separate set of strings; the hammers strike downwards simultaneously on these and on one of the harpsichord's set. Alongside is a clockwork 'recording machine', by which pencil marks record on a long paper roll the pitch and length of notes which are played. *Deutsches Museum, Munich*

164 Pianoforte by Johann Andreas Stein; Augsburg 1797. The light mechanism invented by Stein came to be known as the Viennese action. Mozart much admired the clear and even sound of Stein's instruments, and no heavier kind of piano can realize adequately the exquisite balance between strings and keyboard of early classical chamber music. *Kunsthistorisches Museum, Vienna*

165 Details of three pages from the standard English oboe tutor of the last quarter of the 18th century

   a Title page. Mr Fischer was J. C. Fischer, celebrated oboist of whose vibrato Mozart disapproved.

   b Finger chart

   c Frontispiece, generally said to be a portrait of Fischer. The oboe is the undecorated type common in England after 1750.

New
and Complete Instructions
FOR THE
OBOE or HOBOY

Containing the easiest & most improv'd Rules for Learners to Play;
To which is added
A select collection of Airs, Marches, Minuets, Duets, &c.
also the favorite Rondeau perform'd at Vauxhall, by

Mr FISCHER.

Price 1.6ᵈ

LONDON
Printed & sold by F. Cahusac opposite St Clements Church Yard, Strand

165a

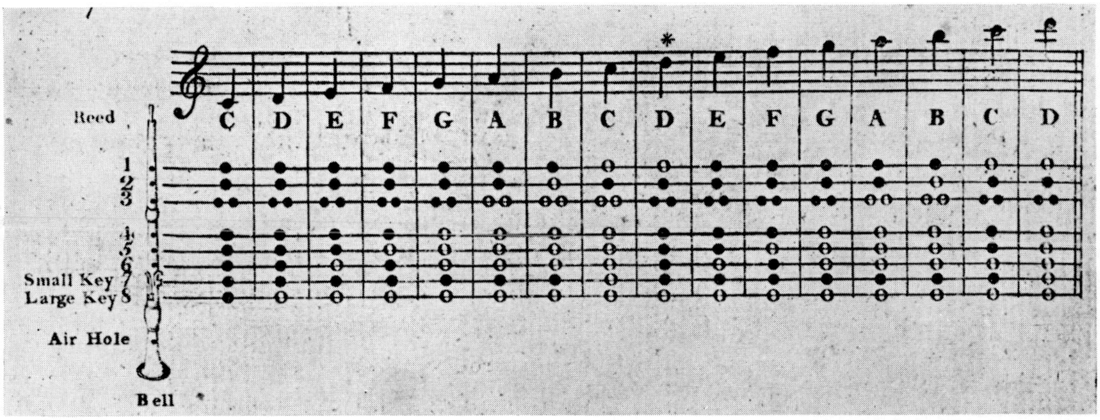

Reed

C D E F G A B C D E F G A B C D

1
2
3
4
5
6
7
Small Key 8
Large Key

Air Hole

Bell

165b

165c

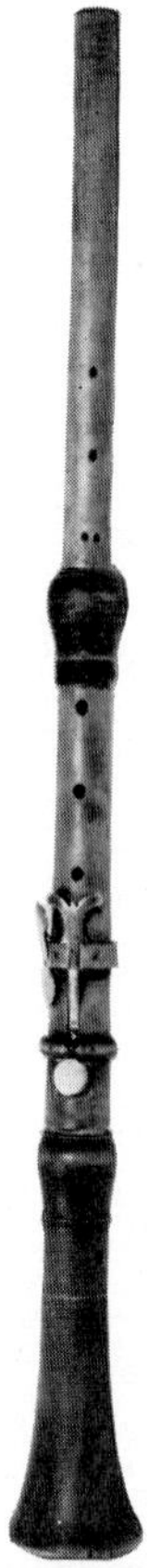

166

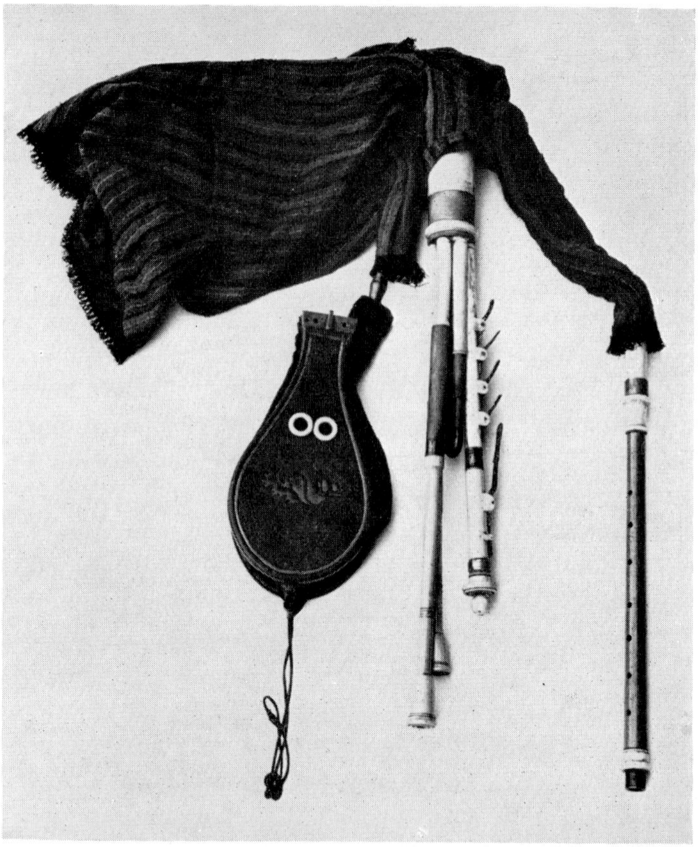

167

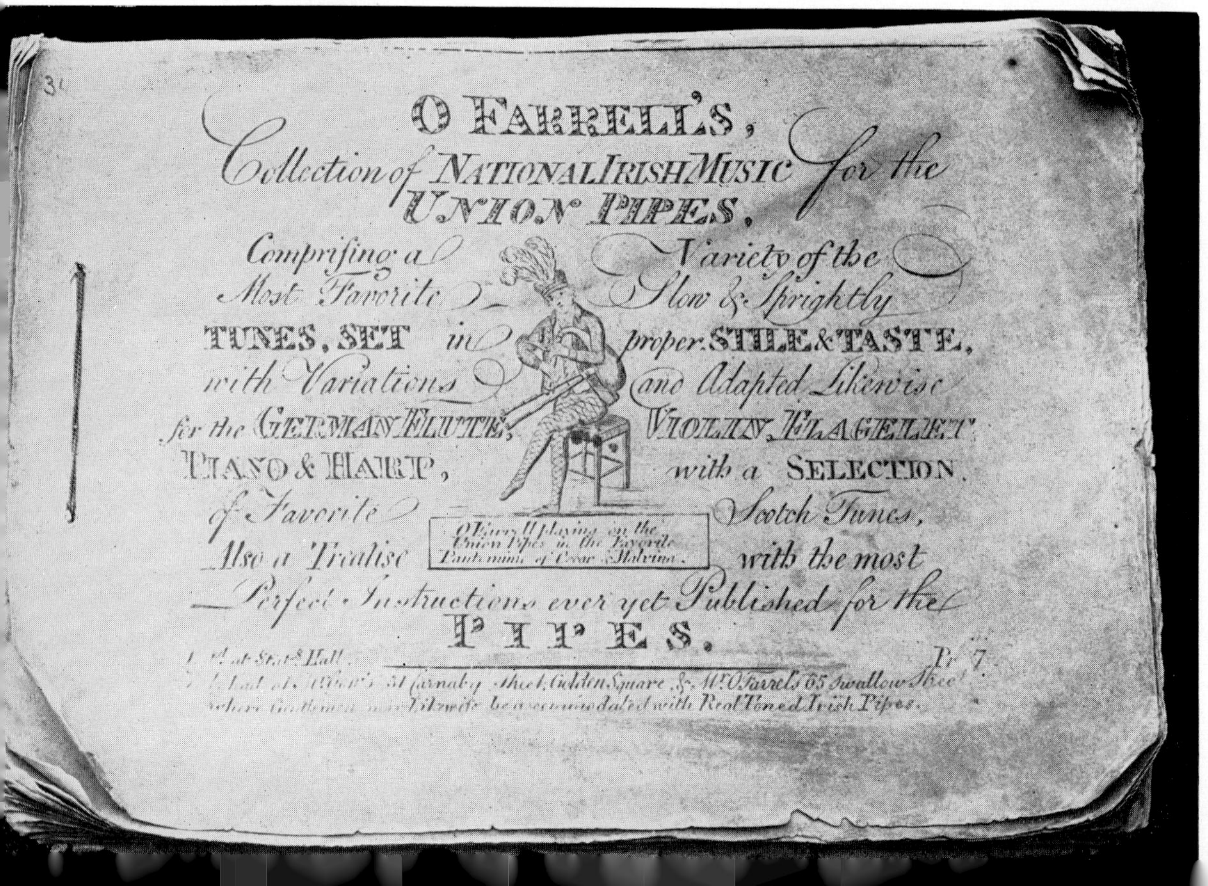

3

O FARRELL'S,

Collection of NATIONAL IRISH MUSIC for the UNION PIPES,

Comprising a Variety of the Most Favorite Slow & Sprightly TUNES, SET in proper STILE & TASTE, with Variations and Adapted Likewise for the GERMAN FLUTE, VIOLIN, FLAGELET, PIANO & HARP, with a SELECTION of Favorite Scotch Tunes, Also a Treatise with the most Perfect Instructions ever yet Published for the

PIPES.

O'Farrell playing on the Union Pipes in the Favorite Pantomime of Oscar & Malvina.

Ent.d at Stat.s Hall. Pr 7

Published at Mr. ...'s 31 Carnaby Street, Golden Square & Mr. O'Farrel's 65 Swallow Street where Gentlemen may likewise be accommodated with Real Toned Irish Pipes.

168

169

170

166 Oboe by Kusder, London, late 18th century, of the type illustrated in plate 165 *b* and *c*
Pitt Rivers Museum, Oxford

167 Irish Union (or Uilleann) pipes by Egan; 1768. The earliest Union pipes had one chanter and two drones. By the middle of the 18th century there were three drones and a regulator – a closed-end pipe with keys (here seen in profile) which the player flicks with his wrist to give changing chords.
National Museum of Ireland, Dublin

168 Title page of O'Farrell's tutor for the Union pipes. O'Farrell describes the regulator in his text, but the illustration is of the old two-drone, no-regulator pipes. *National Museum of Ireland, Dublin*

169 Square piano and cello in 'The Cowper and Gore Families' by John Zoffany (*c* 1734–1810). The cello is gripped between the player's knees and he holds the bow with a fingers-on-the-hair grip.
The Honourable Lady Salmond

170 'Travelling Musicians' by Zoffany. These are of a very different social order from the stately amateurs in plate 169. The low-held fiddles, the cello across the knees, bowed with an underhand hold like the earlier viols, and the large tambourine suggest that this picture was painted before Zoffany, who was a native of Bohemia, came to England. *Pinakoteca, Parma*

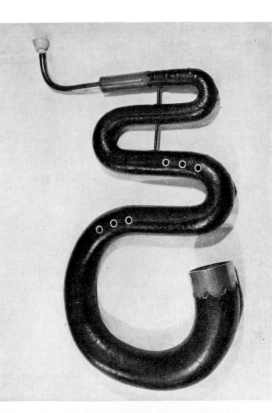

171   172

Double Drums. Drums. Tower Drums.

Trumpets / Trumpets / Trumpets / Trumpets / Tenors / Tenors / Tenors

Organ

Trombonis / Cornos / Cornos / Tenors / Tenors

Cornets / Cornets / Cornos / Cornos / Tenors / Tenors

1st Violins / 1st Violins / 1st Violins / 1st Violins / 1st Violins / 1st Violins / 1st Violins
2d Violins / 2d Violins / 2d Violins / 2d Violins / 2d Violins / 2d Violins / 2d Violins

Voices / Voices / Voices / Voices / Voices / Voices / Voices
Oboes / Oboes / Oboes / Pl Oboes / Pl Oboes
D. Bass / D. Bass / Pl Violoncellos / Organ Keys / Pl Violoncellos / D. Bass / D. Bass
Double Basses / Violoncellos / J. Bates Esqr Conductor / Double Basses / Violoncellos
Double Basses / Violoncellos / Dl. Bassoon / Double Basses / Violoncellos

Pl Bassoons / Pl Bassoons / Bassoons / Bassoons

Second / Second / Second / Second / Second / Second
Bass Voices / Bass Voices / Tenor Voices / Tenor Voices / Alto Voices / Alto Voices

First Bass / First Bass / First Bass / First Tenor / First Tenor / First Tenor / First Alto Voices / First Alto Voices / Alto Voices

1st Cantos / 1st Cantos / 1st Cantos / 2d Cantos / 2d Cantos / 2d Cantos / Cantos / Cantos
First Principal Canto Voices / Second Canto Voices / Principal Singers

Plan of the Orchestra, and Disposition of the Band.

a

1 Cittern, or 'English guitar', by Rauche; London 1770. Wire-strung citterns of various sizes and shapes remained popular as amateur instruments right up to the end of the 18th century. Their tuning made simple chord formations lie easily under the hand, and no skilled technique was needed to produce their cheerful sound. *Ashmolean Museum, Oxford*

2 English keyless serpent of the type shown in plate 172. The English serpent was more compactly folded than the French (see plate 123d). Its unique, glassy sound was still heard in rural church bands in Thomas Hardy's time. Its chief use in the 18th century was in military bands. *Joan Rimmer*

3 'The Sharp Family on the Thames at Fulham' by Zoffany. This fine posed picture shows cello, serpent, two oboes, a pair of horns and a pair of clarinets lying on the small harpsichord, and a theorbo. The last,

played by an elderly member of the family, was long out-of-date. The actual oboes, clarinets and horns shown in this picture are still in existence. *Miss Olive Lloyd-Baker*

174 The 'Musical Performance in Westminster Abbey in Commemoration of Handel' which took place in 1784 was a vast operation involving an enormous chorus and orchestra. It set the pattern for the oversized performances of Handel which went on in England even into the present century.

a Seating plan of the chorus and orchestra. It can be seen from this how far away is this kind of performance, with its additional horns and trombones and massed instruments on every part, from Handel's original intentions. The orchestras for which Handel wrote were similar to that shown in plate 153.

174b

174 *b* View of the orchestra and chorus in Westminster Abbey

175a

175b

176

175 Two English military bands in the 'Ceremony from St James's to St Paul's on Tuesday, the 15th December, 1797, on which day their *Majesties* together with both *Houses of Parliament* went in Solemn Procession to return thanks for the *Naval Victories* obtained by the *British Fleet* over those of France, Spain and Holland'.

a Long drum beaten with two sticks, side drum, clarinet, alto clarinet and horns. The horns in both bands are being played in hunting-horn style.

b Clarinets, alto clarinet, bassoon and horn, preceded by a long or Turkish drum, beaten with a stick and switch

176 Mounted band of the *École Nationale de Musique Militaire* at Versailles; 1805. It consists of two trumpets, two horns played with the hand-in-the-bell technique, two clarinets and two bassoons.

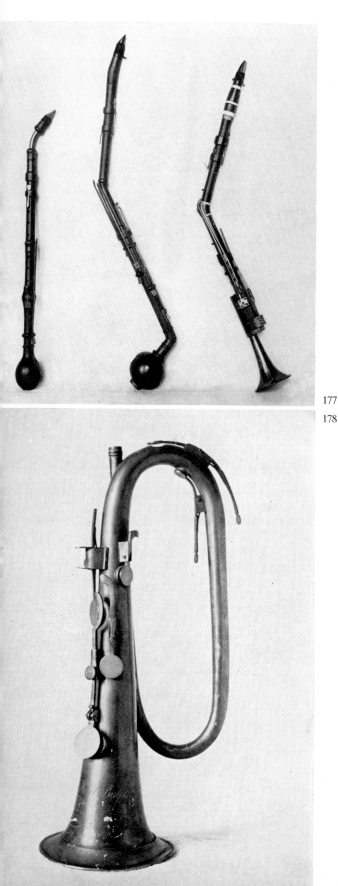

177 Clarinet d'amore and two basset-horns (narrow-bored alto clarinets with additional low notes); *c* 1800. The basset-horn was used to great effect by Mozart, both in small wind ensembles and in opera as an obbligato instrument. It was a popular solo instrument around 1800, and survived in German wind bands right through the 19th century.

Deutsches Museum, Munich

178 Keyed trumpet by William Sandbach; London 1812. The placing of key-covered holes on the tube was a short-lived method of giving the trumpet a chromatic compass. The keyed trumpet, first made in Vienna, was the instrument for which Haydn's trumpet concerto was written. (Mouthpiece is not shown.)

Royal Military School of Music, London

179 The *Royal Patent Kent Bugle*, by Ellard; Dublin 1818. The five-keyed bugle was designed in 1810 by Joseph Halliday, bandmaster of the Cavan Militia, and named after the Duke of Kent, commander-in-chief of the British army. John Distin, soloist in the band of the Grenadier Guards from 1814 onwards, achieved international fame as a virtuoso player of the keyed bugle.

R. Morley Pegge

177

179

178

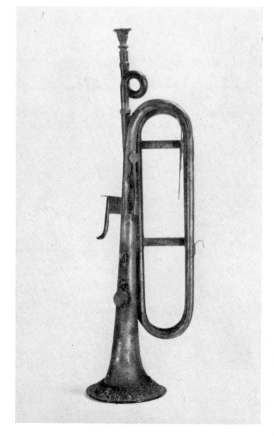

180 Single-action pedal harp by Lerate of Cadiz
Municipal Museum of Music, Barcelona

181 Dital harp by Egan; Dublin 1819. This small neo-Irish
   harp was invented by Egan at a time of strong Irish
   national feeling. The old Irish harp was already
   extinct. This small, portable, gut-strung instrument
   had a curved forepillar and string-shortening mechanism similar to that of the big pedal harp but worked
   by levers set into the forepillar. It was used to accompany the new romantic settings of Irish folk song – a
   use quite alien to the old Irish harp.
   Metropolitan Museum of Art, New York

180

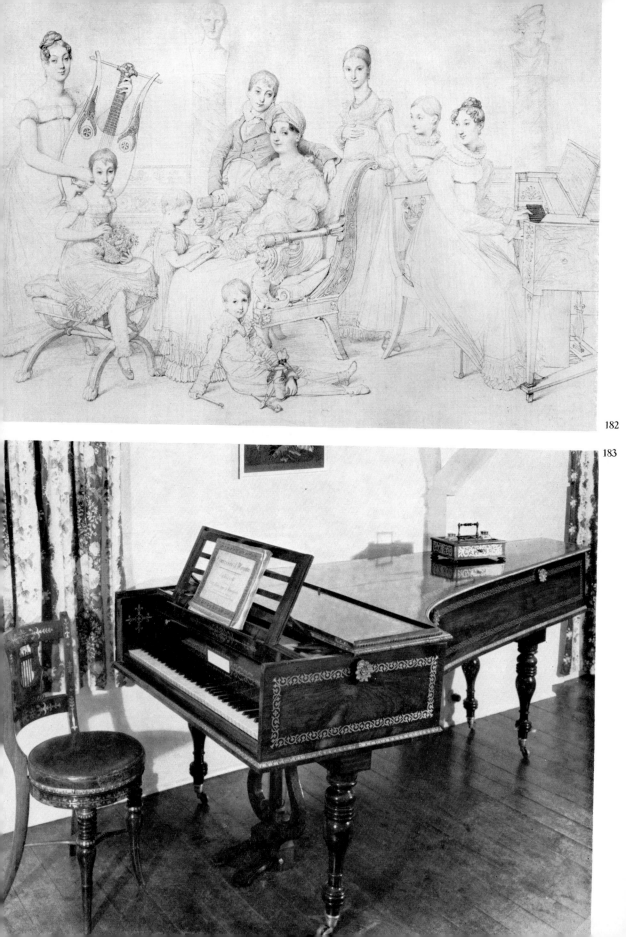

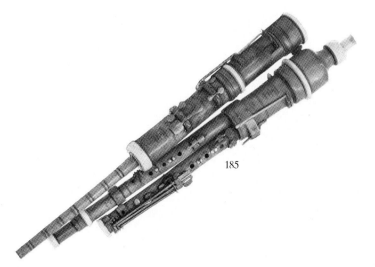

184

185

182 The family of Lucien Bonaparte, by Ingres (1780–1867). The 'lyre-guitar' shown here is one of a family of hybrids, including 'harp-guitars', 'harp-lutes', 'harp-lute-guitars', which were invented in the early part of the 19th century for amateur use.
Grenville L. Winthrop Bequest
Fogg Art Museum, Harvard University

183 Grand pianoforte by John Broadwood; London 1820. This six-octave instrument, with *forte* pedal divided so that it can be used on bass or treble alone, as well as over the whole compass, is almost identical with the Broadwood piano supplied to Beethoven in 1818.
C. F. Colt

184 Violin by Stradivarius, commonly called 'La Messie', fitted with new neck and fingerboard in the 19th century   *Ashmolean Museum, Oxford*

185 Triple flageolet by Bainbridge; London early 19th century. The English flageolet, a recorder-like instrument with a narrow bone tube mouthpiece, was much played by amateurs in the early years of the 19th century for quadrilles and dance music generally. Both single and double flageolets were common; the triple flageolet was something of a freak.
Boosey and Hawkes

186 Guitar by Grobert of Mirecourt. This instrument was given by Paganini to Berlioz, who in turn gave it to the Museum of the Paris Conservatoire, of which he was curator. Berlioz must have been an accomplished guitarist; while in Italy in 1831 he often improvised for local dancers and singers. When he destroyed most of his family papers and relics on the death of his son in 1867, he kept only the baton given him by Mendelssohn and this guitar.

   a Front view

   b Detail showing the signatures of Paganini and Berlioz   *Museum of the Conservatoire, Paris*

186b

186a

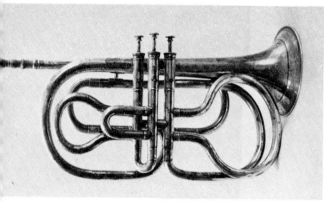

187

188

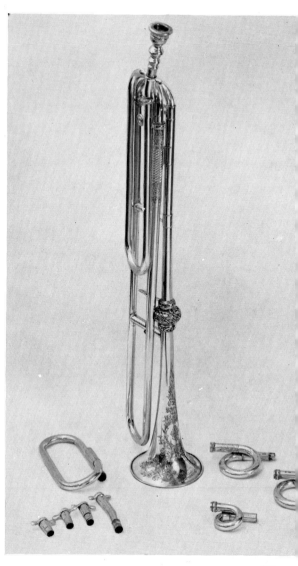

189

187 Valve trumpet with three Stölzel piston valves. The invention of valves seems to have taken place in Germany about 1815; the Silesian horn player Heinrich Stölzel, after whom valves of the type shown here are called, is generally credited with the invention.

R. Morley Pegge

188 French horn with three rotary valves by W. Glier; Warsaw 1835. The rotary valve, probably invented by Joseph Riedl of Vienna in the early 1830s, was an efficient mechanism in which extra tubing was connected to the horn by a revolving cylinder. The

rotary valves in use today are the same in all essentials as those introduced in 1832. *R. Morley Pegge*

189 Silver slide trumpet with additional crooks and shanks by Kohler and Son; London mid-19th century. A trumpet with a small looped slide which gave a range of contiguous notes not available on the natural trumpet was used in England through most of the 19th century while valved instruments were coming into general use elsewhere. This slide trumpet belonged to Thomas Harper (1816–98), state trumpeter to Queen Victoria. *Boosey and Hawkes*

190 The Distin family with saxhorns made for them in 1844 by Adolphe Sax. These valved brass instruments, with a bore roughly like a bugle, were patented by Sax (though not invented by him) in 1845, and instruments of this type have been used in all brass bands and in many continental military bands ever since. They were introduced into England by John Distin and his sons, who had a brass quintet.

191 'Rehearsal before Mass' by Soyer (1823–1903). The bass part is being played on an ophicleide, a keyed brass instrument which succeeded the serpent and was for a time co-existent with the modern tuba, or valved brass bass.

190

191

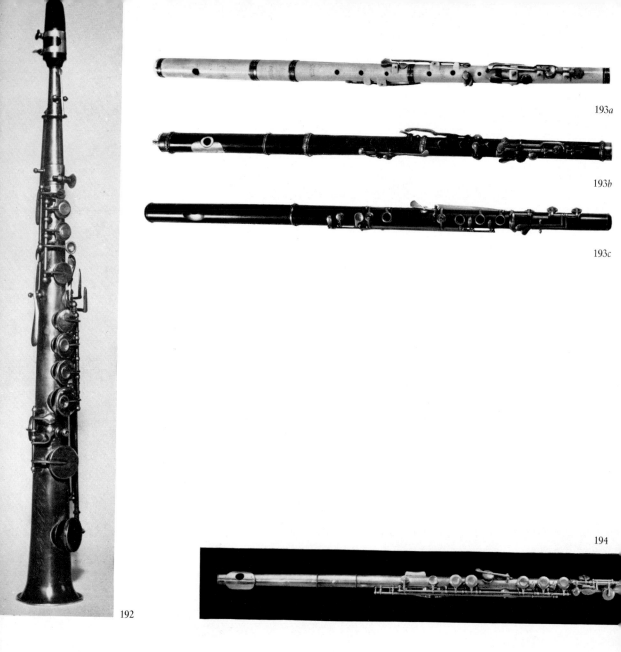

192

193a

193b

193c

194

192 Soprano saxophone by Adolphe Sax; Paris 1855–8. Sax almost certainly had the military band in mind when experimenting, but the powerful and thick sound of the saxophones has proved effective in many kinds of music. *Horniman Museum, London*

193 Three conical flutes

  a Eight-keyed ivory flute by Drouet; London 1815–19. This is the typical small-holed instrument of the early 19th-century flute virtuosi.

  b 'Nicholson's Improved' flute by T. Prowse; London 1820–2. This is the large-holed model designed by Charles Nicholson (1795–1837), the distinguished English flautist.

  c Conical flute by Theobald Boehm; Munich 1832. The first Boehm flute had a conical bore, but

drastically redesigned keywork, with open 'rings' over the finger-holes which enabled the finger covering the hole also to work a distant key which was connected to the ring by a long rotating rod. Mechanism working on this principle was eventually applied to all woodwind instruments.

Horniman Museum, London

194 Cylindrical silver flute with gold lip-plate and gold springs by Theobald Boehm; Munich c 1860. Boehm's completely redesigned flute, patented in 1847, had the cylindrical bore of the pre-Hotteterre flutes with a parabolic head joint. The very large holes were covered by padded keys. The flute universally used today (except in certain flute and drum bands) is, in all essentials, this instrument. *Philip Bate*

Thirteen-keyed oboe by Koch; Vienna c 1825. The tuning slide at the top – an overall pitch-changing device not usually found on the oboe – is extended. The advanced model of the 1820s was this oboe, designed by the Viennese player Josef Sellner and illustrated in his tutor. The present-day Viennese oboe, now little used except in Vienna and to some extent in Russia, is much the same as this instrument.

Philip Bate

Two Triébert-system oboes. Although the first mechanization of the oboe took place in Germany and Austria, the modern fully keyed oboe was the creation of French makers, just as the original two-keyed oboe had been. Between 1840 and 1880 the Triébert family and their craftsmen refined the bore of the instrument and progressively developed the system of keywork into that used today.

a Boxwood oboe with brass keys (basically Triébert Système A4) by Triébert; Paris c 1848

b African blackwood oboe with German silver keys (Triébert Système 5) by Morton and Sons; London 1872–83   *Philip Bate*

Cor Anglais Moderne by Henri Brod; Paris 1839. The 18th-century tenor oboe known as the cor anglais (a name whose origin is obscure) was originally a somewhat cumbersome instrument, semicircular or angled in form. A straight cor anglais, comparable in design with the contemporary French oboe, and prototype of the modern instrument, was designed by the French oboist and maker Henri Brod, and exhibited at the Paris Exhibition of 1839.

Boosey and Hawkes

195   196a   196b

197

1

202a, b

198 Two twelve-keyed clarinets by Key; London c 1825. These boxwood clarinets were played in the earlier part of his professional life by the English virtuoso Henry Lazarus (1815–95). The keys turn on pins set into wooden ridges raised on the body of the instrument.
Boosey and Hawkes

199 Thirteen-keyed boxwood clarinet by Boosé; London 1851. This clarinet, exhibited at the Great Exhibition of 1851, has decorated silver mounts and keys. As in the Triébert oboes and the Brod *cor anglais moderne*, the keywork is set on pillars driven directly into the wood.
Boosey and Hawkes

200 Boehm-system clarinet, shown without mouthpiece, by Boosey and Hawkes; London c 1900. This was made for Manuel Gomez (1859–1930), first principal clarinettist of the London Symphony Orchestra.
Boosey and Hawkes

201 Symphonium by Sir Charles Wheatstone; London 1829. European free-reed instruments, sounding with small metal tongues fixed at one end into a frame in which they vibrate freely, date only from the first

quarter of the 19th century. Interest in the ancient 'mouthorgans' of the Far East (Chinese *sheng*, Japanese *sho*) is thought to have prompted the experiments, simultaneously carried out in France, England and Germany, which led eventually to the mouth-blown harmonica and the bellows-blown concertina, harmonium and accordion. The symphonium was blown through the hole in the front. The push buttons are of ivory and the reeds of gold.
James Howarth

202 a Eleven-keyed bassoon by Savary jeune; Paris 1829. (The wing joint is a replacement.)

b Sixteen-keyed Almanraeder bassoon by Schott; Mainz 1823–31. There were two different trends in bassoon design from the 1820s onwards. The French bassoon, while having keys added to it, retained the colourful character of the 18th-century instrument. In Germany the instrument's basic design was considerably altered. The French bassoon is still magnificently played in France, Belgium and Italy. Elsewhere the German, or Heckel, bassoon is generally used. *Horniman Museum, London*

203

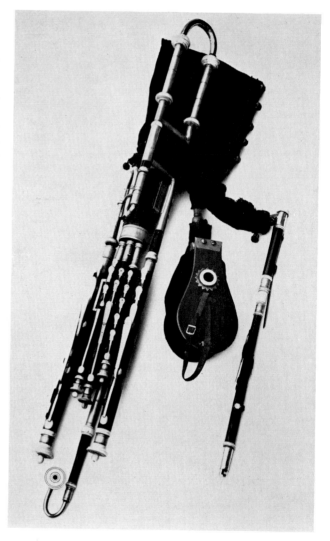

204

205

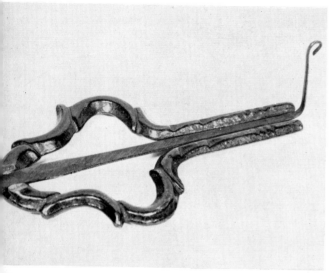

203 Sean Ryan, Dublin publican, playing the concertina. The free-reed instruments have rarely found a place in art music. They have been used in all kinds of popular music, from Victorian parlour hymn accompanying to the Dublin 'singing pubs' and the folk bands of the Caucasus.

Messrs Arthur Guinness, Son and Co Ltd, Dublin

204 Irish Union pipes by Moloney; Kilrush 1838. These Irish pipes, fitted with many regulators (see plates 167 and 168), have been scornfully called 'harmoniums' by Scottish pipers. *National Museum of Ireland, Dublin*

205 Silver Jew's harp; 19th century. German instruments of this type, with a tongue which is plucked while the frame is held close to the mouth which acts as a resonator, are widely distributed among primitive peoples. Silver Jew's harps were in great demand by courting youths in Austria in the 19th century. The tiny sound was considered to be particularly persuasive. *Pitt Rivers Museum, Oxford*

206 Liszt's music room at Weimar. The constructional
features which differentiate the heavy modern grand
from the lighter piano of Beethoven's day were all
introduced during Liszt's lifetime (1811–86). The metal
frame and cross stringing can be seen on this Bechstein
piano which was used by Liszt in his later years.
Liszt's House, Weimar

207 A candidate playing the three-stringed double-bass
before a jury at the Paris Conservatoire, *c* 1880, drawn
by Paul Renouard (1845–1924). The jury includes
Ambroise Thomas, director of the Conservatoire,
sitting behind the tuning fork, and Gounod, Massenet
and Delibes. *Luxembourg Palace, Paris*

206

207

209

210

208

208 Sir Edward Burne-Jones's piano, by Broadwood of London. The case was designed by William Morris.
Victoria and Albert Museum, London (Crown copyright)

209 'Wagner Tubas' by Alexander; Mainz late 19th century. These are not true tubas, but French horn-saxhorn hybrids, made at Wagner's suggestion to produce what he felt to be a missing kind of brass tone. Wagner himself wrote for them only in *The Ring*. Bruckner and Richard Strauss used them occasionally, but they have never come into general use. *Boosey and Hawkes*

210 Heckelphone by Heckel, Biebrich-am-Rhein; 20th century. This large-bored instrument, sounding an octave below the oboe, should not be confused with the narrow-bored French baritone oboe. Like the 'Wagner tuba', it was made at Wagner's suggestion though it did not appear until after his death. Strauss wrote for it in *Salome* and *Elektra* and there is an excellent trio with viola and piano by Hindemith. It is now used to some extent in incidental music for films, radio and television, a sphere in which most instruments of unusual sonority are exploited.
Wilhelm Heckel

211 'Young Girls at the Piano' by Renoir (1841–1919). By the middle of the 19th century the upright piano had supplanted the square as a domestic instrument. Many households still possess upright pianos in heavy candle-bracketed cases like that in Renoir's picture.
The Louvre, Paris (© SPADEM, Paris 1964)

◄ 211

212 London street musicians, with pedal harp, violin, cornet and three-stringed bass; 1884. Itinerant musicians, who never play from written music, often preserve musical practices long after they have disappeared from more formal musical circles.

From O. J. Morris Grandfather's London *1961*

213 Russian *rozhok* band; late 19th century. The *rozhok*, now rare in Russia, is a folk instrument similar to the mute cornett which was a high art instrument in the West in the 16th and 17th centuries. The traditional material for the *rozhok* is juniper wood bound round with birch bark, but unbound palmwood is also used.

State Central Museum of Musical Culture, Moscow

1918 onwards

214

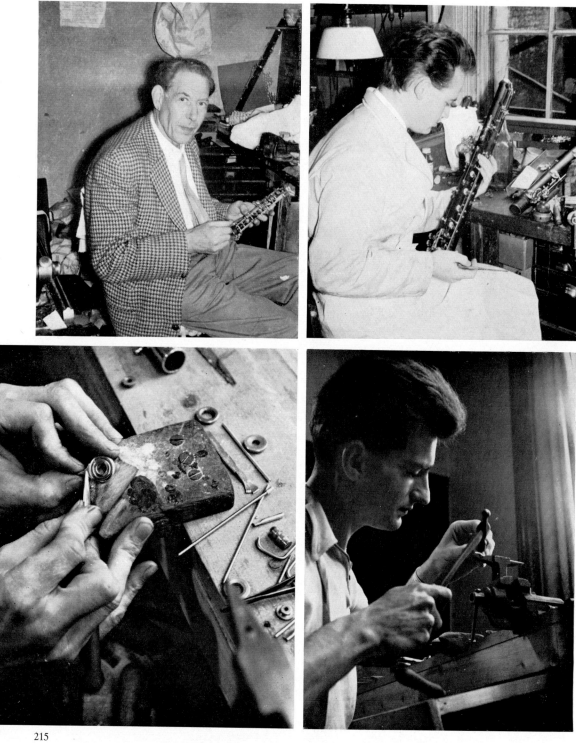

14 Members of the family firm of George Howarth and Son, London, who have been making and repairing instruments for three generations. Left, James Howarth, the present proprietor; right, Paul Howarth, the proprietor's son, adjusting the mechanism of a Boehm bassoon, part of the family's collection of old instruments.

15 Craftsmen of the Flutemakers' Guild of London at work on flutes. While mass-production methods can be used for the manufacture of cheaper instruments, the highest grades of woodwind can be produced only by craftsmen working by hand. The Flutemakers' Guild was formed with the assistance of the then Lord Mayor of London, Sir Bernard Waley-Cohen, and C. S. Padgett of the Worshipful Company of Goldsmiths, to maintain the high traditional standards of English flutemaking and to enable young craftsmen to be trained.

16 Large-scale manufacture of clarinets in the Edgware factory of Messrs Boosey and Hawkes. Left, *Dalbergia melonoxolon* (African blackwood) imported in bulk from Tanganyika; right, the inspection of bored joints.

17 Processes in the manufacture of brass instruments at Messrs Boosey and Hawkes' factory: right, pegging out the flare on large trombone bells; below, general view of the brass workshop.

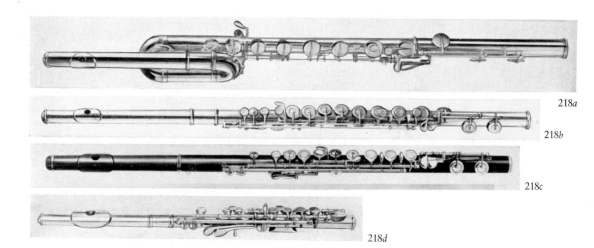

218a

218b

218c

218d

218 *a* Bass flute
   b Alto flute
   c Flute
   d Piccolo   *By Rudall Carte of London*

219 Oboe, oboe d'amore and cor anglais
                    By T. W. Howarth and Company of London

220 The complete range of clarinets from the high A♭
   clarinet to the giant octo-contrabass
                    By G. Leblanc of Paris

219

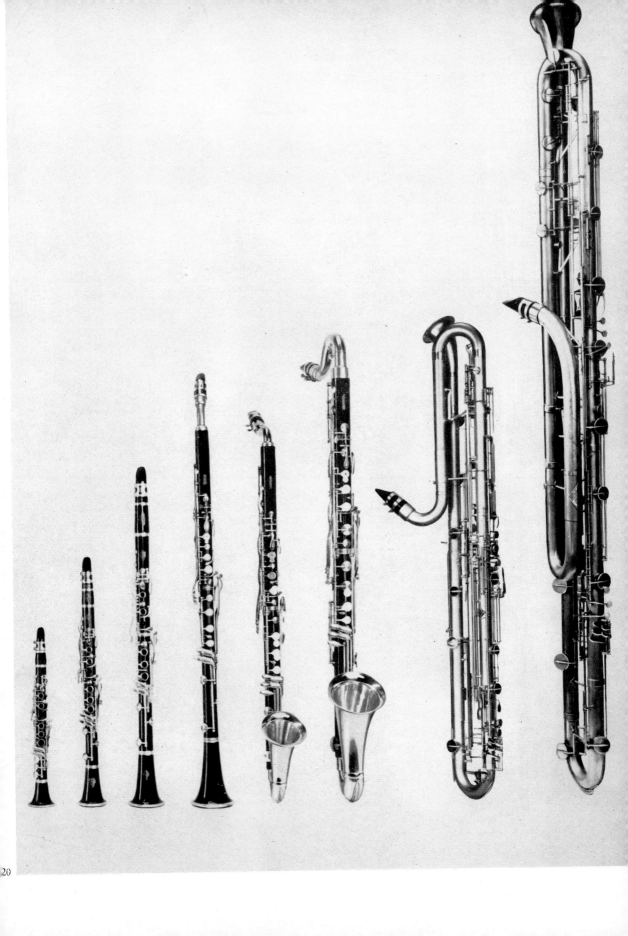

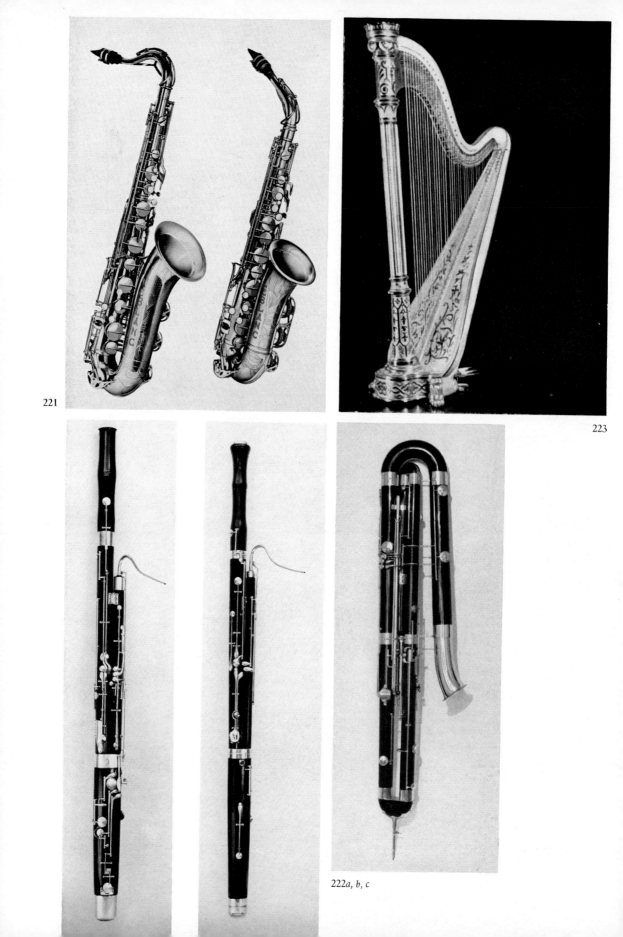

221

223

222a, b, c

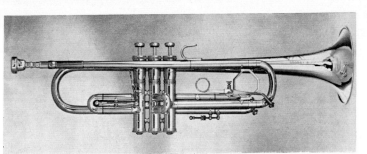

224a

224b

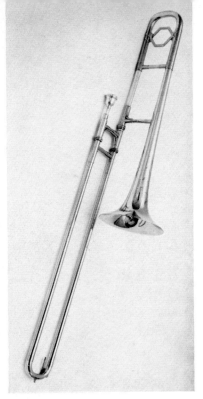

224c

225b

225a

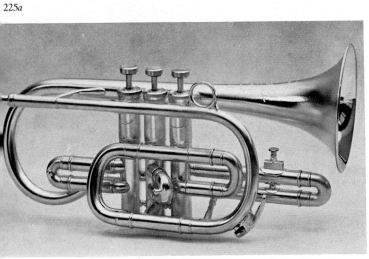

Baritone and alto saxophones of the model 'Le Rationel' designed by Charles Houvenaghel (designer of the contrabass and octo-contrabass clarinets), who devised for them a new system of fingering and key mechanism   *By G. Leblanc of Paris*

2 *a* French or Buffet-system bassoon

By Mahillon of London

b German or Heckel-system bassoon, 'Model 61'

By W. Lewington of London

c Contra-bassoon   *By Lignatone of Prague*

223 Double-action pedal harp with broad soundbox

By Obermayer of Starnberg

224 *a* Trumpet *b* Horn *c* Trombone

By Boosey and Hawkes of London

225 *a* Cornet *b* Tuba   *By Besson of London*

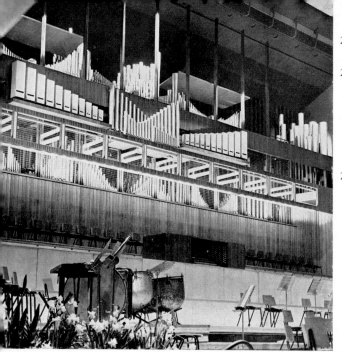

226 Organ of the Royal Festival Hall, London, to a specification by Ralph Downes, completed in 1953. It has
five keyboards – Great, Positive, Swell, Choir and
Solo – and pedals, with a total of one hundred and
three speaking stops. The design is in accord with
modern tendencies towards reviving the tonal
qualities of the late baroque organ and dispensing
with an organ case.   *By Harrison & Harrison of Durham*

227 Violins, viola and cello designed by Lionel Tertis.
The large viola, produced in 1937, was prompted by
the paucity of good instruments and their high price,
and by the poor quality and irrational design of many
of the then current models. Violas after the Tertis
design, which embodies some features also found in
the big violas of the late 16th and early 17th centuries,
are now produced by many makers. The Tertis cello
appeared in 1960, and the violin in 1963. These instruments, with their enlarged resonance chambers, have
a sonority comparable with that of the Tertis violas.
    By Lawrence Cocker of Derby

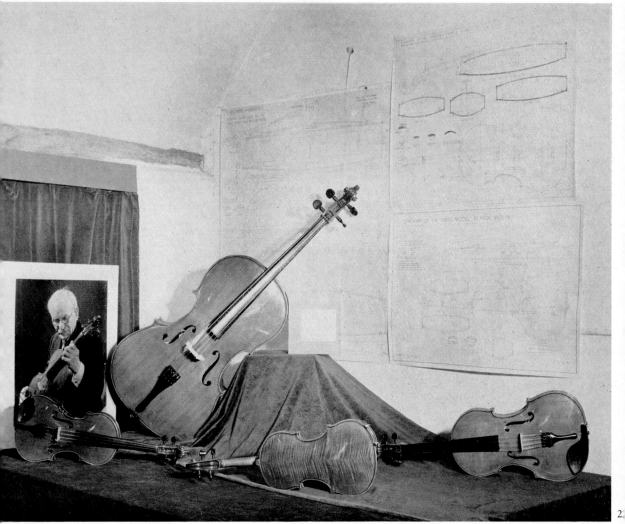

228 Chime bars. These are separate, tuned metal plates over horizontal tube resonators. Invented primarily for elementary teaching purposes, they can be set out in any scale, mode or note sequence, unlike the large orchestral tuned percussion instruments which are always arranged in a piano-keyboard fashion. The function of chime bars recalls that of the early medieval song-school *cymbala*.   *By the London Music Shop, London*

229 *a* Vibraphone. One of the few instruments invented in the 20th century, it consists of tuned slabs of light metal, below which are tube resonators fitted with mechanically or electrically operated fans.

   b Playing detail   *By the Premier Drum Company, London*

230 Pedal *timpani*. These kettle-drums, tuned by mechanism worked from pedals, facilitate quick re-tuning and also provide glissando effects impossible on hand-tuned *timpani*.   *By the Premier Drum Company, London*

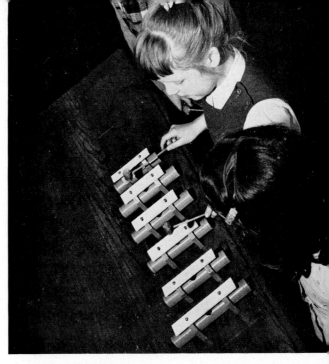

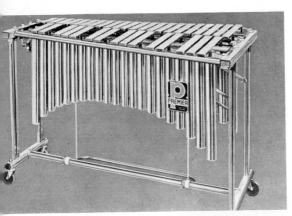

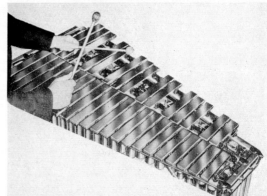

229a, b

230

a   *b*   *c*

d   *e*   *f*   231

232a

232c

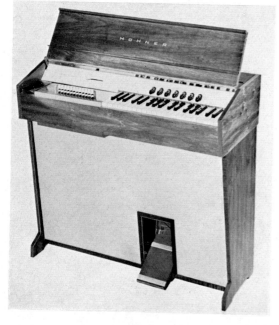

232b

232d

233

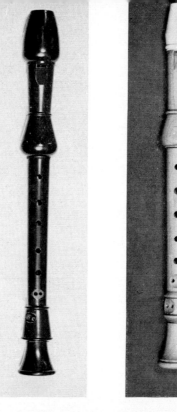

234

231 Latin-American rhythm instruments:

    a Canza – a metal version of a tube rattle

    b Reco-Reco – a scraper

    c Afoche – more commonly called *maraca* in Europe

    d Tamborim, sometimes called cigar box – a single-headed square drum whose tone quality is varied by left hand on and off the skin

    e Cuica – a friction drum

    f Cuica stick

232 *a* Chromatic harmonica

    b Accordion

    c Chord organ

    d Melodica

The chromatic harmonica has a slide lever to sharpen or flatten any note. The accordion has five sets of reeds and twenty-two tone effects. The organ which is, in effect, a non-portable and automatically blown accordion, has three sets of reeds and seven register switches. The recently invented melodica, with beak-shaped mouthpiece and piano-type keys, is primarily an educational instrument.   *By Hohner of Trossingen*

233 Concert guitar   *By Clifford Essex of London*

234 Descant recorders in (left) plastic and (right) wood
    By Schott of London

235 Steel guitar. This instrument is generally said to be derived from the flat-on-the-knees style in which the natives of Hawaii played the ordinary guitar which was introduced to them by American sailors. It now bears a closer resemblance in type to European and Appalachian folk fretted zithers, though its powerful and electrically magnified tone quality is far removed from them.

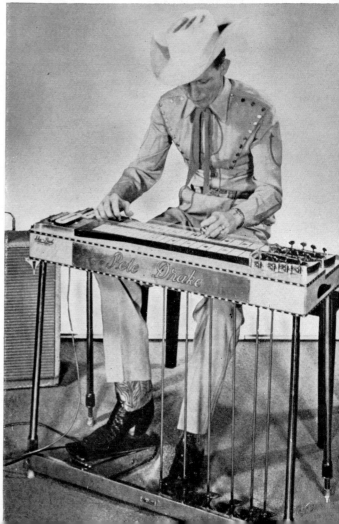

235

238

239

236 Zouave band. Typical instruments of the large French military band are played in the band of this Colonial regiment.

237 Members of a Gurkha pipe band. Scottish bagpipes and their characteristic musical idiom have had a remarkable fascination for non-Scottish people, and pipers from many parts of the world now rival native Scots in expertise.

238 Fiddle of orange-box wood, made and played by B. Dunne, street musician, of Cork, Ireland

239 Limousin regional band of violin, hurdy-gurdy (*vielle*), bagpipe (*cabrette*) and button-accordion

240 Italian *zampogna*, with bag made from the inner tube of a tyre instead of the traditional whole animal skin

240

241

242

243

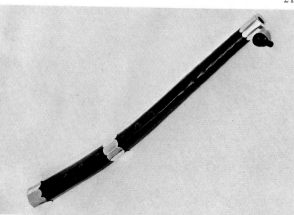

241 Keyboard instrument room at the Deutsches Museum, Munich. Most of the instruments are in working order and appropriate music is played on them by a uniformed attendant.

242 Reproduction of a bandora based on measurements given by Praetorius (1619) and James Talbot (late 17th century)   *By Donald Gill of London 1961*

243 Reproduction of a *cornettino* (dated 1518)
          By Christopher Monk of Hindhead, Surrey, 1963

244 Modern harpsichord and clavichord
          By John Challis of Detroit, U S.A.

245 Modern chamber organ, of the size and style of a baroque chamber organ   *By N. P. Mander of London*

246 Reproduction of a Viennese fortepiano
          By Hugh Gough of London

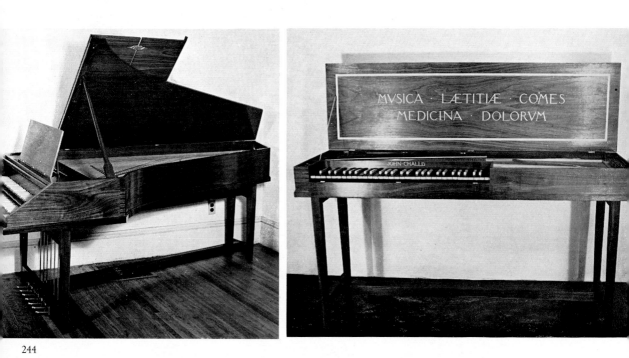

244

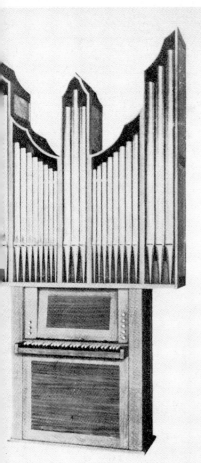

245

246

247 Electronic Sound Synthesiser at the Columbia-Princeton Electronic Music Center, Columbia University, New York. Milton Babbitt, one of the composers working in the Electronic Music Center, has provided the following description: 'The Mark II R.C.A. Electronic Sound Synthesiser, designed by Dr Harry Olson and Mr Herbert Belar, is an instrument for the completely electronic specification, generation and regulation of every value of the sound event, and the mode of progression from such a sound event to the next so specified event.'

248 Six- and seven-year-olds at the Brampton Infant School, East Ham, Middlesex, playing recorders, triangle, beaten cymbal, tambourine, side drum, chime bars and glockenspiel

Acknowledgments

1 By permission of the Musée de l'Homme, Paris
2 By permission of the Pitt Rivers Museum, Oxford
3 By permission of the Jutland Archaeological Society, Aarhus, Denmark,
4–7 By permission of the Pitt Rivers Museum, Oxford
8 Authors
9, 10 By permission of the Pitt Rivers Museum, Oxford
11 By courtesy of the National Museum of Ireland, Dublin
12 Hirmer Verlag, Munich
13 By courtesy of the National Museum of Ireland, Dublin
14, 15 By courtesy of the Ashmolean Museum, Oxford
16 Foto Marburg
17 By permission of the Pitt Rivers Museum, Oxford
18 By courtesy of the Ashmolean Museum, Oxford
19 By the courtesy of the Trustees of the British Museum, London
20 By courtesy of the Ashmolean Museum, Oxford
21 Mansell-Alinari
22 Mansell-Anderson
23 By courtesy of H.W.Janson
24 Mansell-Alinari
25 By courtesy of the Trustees of the British Museum, London
26 By courtesy of the Deutsches Museum, Munich
27 By permission of the Pitt Rivers Museum, Oxford
28 Mansell-Anderson
29 By courtesy of the Pontifical Commission for Sacred Archaeology, Rome
30, 31 By permission of the Pitt Rivers Museum, Oxford
32, 33 By courtesy of the Trustees of the British Museum, London
34 By courtesy of the Commissioners of Public Works in Ireland
35 Roger-Viollet, Paris
36 By courtesy of the Bibliothèque Nationale, Paris
37, 38 By courtesy of Canon Charles Barberis
39 By courtesy of the Bibliothèque Nationale, Paris
40 By permission of the Pitt Rivers Museum, Oxford
41 By courtesy of the Master and Fellows of St John's College, Cambridge
42, 43 By permission of the Pitt Rivers Museum, Oxford
44 By courtesy of the University of Glasgow
45 By permission of the Caisse Nationale des Monuments Historiques, Paris
46 By courtesy of Léon Violet, Gard, France
47 By courtesy of the Trustees of the British Museum, London
48 By permission of the Caisse Nationale des Monuments Historiques, Paris
49 By permission of the University of Heidelberg
50 By permission of the Pitt Rivers Museum, Oxford
51 By permission of Corpus Christi College, Cambridge, and the Courtauld Institute of Art, London
52 By courtesy of the National Museum of Wales, Cardiff
53 By permission of the Pitt Rivers Museum, Oxford
54 By courtesy of the Trustees of the British Museum, London
55 By permission of the Pitt Rivers Museum, Oxford
56 By courtesy of the Trustees of the British Museum, London
57 Mansell-Alinari
58 By courtesy of the Metropolitan Museum of Art, New York
59 By courtesy of the Trustees of the British Museum, London
60 By courtesy of the Curators of the Bodleian Library, Oxford
61 By permission of the Caisse Nationale des Monuments Historiques, Paris
62 By courtesy of the Curators of the Bodleian Library, Oxford
63 By courtesy of the Bibliothèque Royale, Brussels
64 By courtesy of the Metropolitan Museum of Art, New York
65 By courtesy of Thames and Hudson (from *Byzantine Frescoes and Icons in Yugoslavia* by Oto Bihalji-Merin and Svetislav Mandić)
66 By courtesy of the Curators of the Bodleian Library, Oxford
67 By permission of the Caisse Nationale des Monuments Historiques, Paris
68 By permission of the Gordon Fraser Gallery, London (photograph by Edwin Smith)
69 By permission of the Collection Haags, Gemeentemuseum, The Hague
70 By courtesy of the Board of Trinity College, Dublin (photograph by courtesy of the Department of Research Laboratory, British Museum, London)
71 By courtesy of the Trustees of the British Museum, London
73 By permission of Wilhelm Castelli, Lübeck
74 By permission of the Pitt Rivers Museum, Oxford
75 Mansell-Alinari
76 By permission of the Pallas Gallery, London
77 By permission of the National Buildings Record, London
78 By courtesy of the National Museum of Wales, Cardiff
79, 80 By permission of Wilhelm Castelli, Lübeck
81 By courtesy of the Ashmolean Museum, Oxford
82 By courtesy of Mario Moretti, Orvieto
83 By permission of Wiechmann-Verlag, Munich
84 Mansell-Alinari
85 By courtesy of the National Gallery of Ireland, Dublin
86 Foto Marburg
87 By courtesy of the Trustees, the National Gallery, London
88 By permission of the Pitt Rivers Museum, Oxford
90 By courtesy of the Kunstmuseum, Basel
96, 97 By permission of the Pitt Rivers Museum, Oxford
98, 99 Mansell-Alinari
100 By permission of the Victoria and Albert Museum, London

101 By permission of the Museum of the Conservatoire, Paris

102 By courtesy of the Worcester Art Museum, Worcester, Massachusetts

103 By courtesy of the Ashmolean Museum, Oxford

106, 107 By permission of the Victoria and Albert Museum, London

108–111 By courtesy of the Ashmolean Museum, Oxford

112 By permission of the National Portrait Gallery, London

113 Mansell-Alinari

114 By courtesy of the Bibliothèque Nationale, Paris

115 By permission of the Museum of the Conservatoire, Brussels

116 By courtesy of the Germanisches National-Museum, Nuremberg

117 By courtesy of the Ashmolean Museum, Oxford

118 By permission of the Museum of Music History, Copenhagen

119 Giraudon, Paris

120 By permission of the Art Gallery of the Prussian State Museums

121 Roger-Viollet, Paris

124 By courtesy of the Metropolitan Museum of Art, New York

125 By permission of the Pitt Rivers Museum, Oxford

126 By courtesy of the Deutsches Museum, Munich

127 By permission of the Museum of the Conservatoire, Paris

128 Authors

129 By courtesy of the Bavarian National Museum, Munich

130 By permission of the Victoria and Albert Museum, London

132 By permission of St Anne's Museum, Lübeck

133 By courtesy of Mrs Cynthia Legh

134 By courtesy of the National Museum of Ireland, Dublin

135 By permission of the Horniman Museum, London

136 By courtesy of the Metropolitan Museum of Art, New York

138 By courtesy of Mr J.M.Taphouse

139 By permission of the Victoria and Albert Museum, London

140 By courtesy of Mrs Nansi Richards Jones

141 By courtesy of the Metropolitan Museum of Art, New York

142, 143 By courtesy of the Bavarian National Museum, Munich

144 By permission of the Collection Haags, Gemeentemuseum, The Hague

145 By permission of the Pitt Rivers Museum, Oxford

146 By permission of Bärenreiter Verlag, Cassel

147 By permission of Knut Aune Kunstforlag, Oslo

148 Roger-Viollet, Paris

150 By permission of the Museum of the Conservatoire, Paris

151 By courtesy of the National Museum of Ireland, Dublin

152 By courtesy of Monsieur Cailleux (photograph by permission of the Royal Academy of Arts, London)

154 By permission of Frost and Reed Ltd, London, owners of the copyright of the mezzotint by Joseph Chamberlain

155, 156 Roger-Viollet, Paris

158 By courtesy of Wilhelm Gerling Verlag, Darmstadt

159 By permission of Frost and Reed Ltd, London, owners of the copyright of the mezzotint by Arthur L. Cox

160 By permission of the Horniman Museum, London

161 By courtesy of the Deutsches Museum, Munich

162 Authors

163 By courtesy of the Deutsches Museum, Munich

164 By permission of the Kunsthistorisches Museum, Vienna

166 By permission of the Pitt Rivers Museum, Oxford

167, 168 By courtesy of the National Museum of Ireland, Dublin

169 By courtesy of The Honourable Lady Salmond (photograph by courtesy of the Royal Academy of Arts, London)

170 Mansell-Alinari

171 By courtesy of the Ashmolean Museum, Oxford

172 Authors

173 By courtesy of Miss Olive Lloyd-Baker (photograph by courtesy of the Royal Academy of Arts, London)

175 By courtesy of Mr Robin Drummond-Hay

176 Roger-Viollet, Paris

177 By courtesy of the Deutsches Museum, Munich

178 By courtesy of the Trustees of the Royal Military School of Music Museum, Kneller Hall, London

179 By courtesy of Mr Reginald Morley Pegge

180 By courtesy of the Municipal Museum of Music, Barcelona

181 By courtesy of the Metropolitan Museum, New York

182 By permission of the Fogg Art Museum, Harvard University

183 By courtesy of Mr C.F.Colt

184 By courtesy of the Ashmolean Museum, Oxford

185 By courtesy of Boosey and Hawkes Ltd, London

186 By permission of the Museum of the Conservatoire, Paris

187, 188 By courtesy of Mr Reginald Morley Pegge

189 By courtesy of Boosey and Hawkes Ltd, London

190 By courtesy of Heffer and Son, Cambridge

191 Roger-Viollet, Paris

192, 193 By permission of the Horniman Museum, London

194–196 By courtesy of Mr Philip Bate

197–200 By courtesy of Boosey and Hawkes Ltd, London

201 By courtesy of Mr James Howarth

202 By permission of the Horniman Museum, London

203 By courtesy of Messrs Arthur Guinness, Son and Company Ltd, Dublin

204 By courtesy of the National Museum of Ireland, Dublin

205 By permission of the Pitt Rivers Museum, Oxford

206 By permission of Nationale Forschungs- und Gedenkstätten in Weimar

207 Roger-Viollet, Paris

208 By permission of the Victoria and Albert Museum, London

209 By courtesy of Boosey and Hawkes Ltd, London

210 By courtesy of Wilhelm Heckel, Biebrich-am-Rhein

211 By permission of the Medici Society, London

212 By permission of Putnam and Company Ltd, London

213 By courtesy of Mr Christopher Monk, and E.N.Alekseeva and K.I.Egorov, State Central Museum of Musical Culture, Moscow

214 By courtesy of Mr James Howarth

215 By courtesy of the Flutemakers' Guild, London
216, 217 By courtesy of Boosey and Hawkes Ltd, London
218 By courtesy of Rudall Carte and Company Ltd, London
219 By courtesy of T.W.Howarth, London
220, 221 By courtesy of Leblanc, Paris
222 By courtesy of Mr William Lewington
223 By courtesy of Obermayer, Starnberg
224, 225 By courtesy of Besson and Company, London
226 By courtesy of the Royal Festival Hall, London
227 By courtesy of Mr Lionel Tertis
228 By courtesy of the Premier Drum Company, London
229 By courtesy of Miss Winifred Stevens and the Education Committee of the County Borough of East Ham (photograph by courtesy of Fotofare, London)
230 By courtesy of the Premier Drum Company, London
231 By courtesy of Fermato do Brasil and Mills Music Limited, London
232 By courtesy of Hohner Concessionaires, London

233 By courtesy of Clifford Essex, London
234 By courtesy of Schott and Company Ltd, London
235 By courtesy of the Decca Record Company Ltd
236 Roger-Viollet, Paris
237 By permission of *The Scotsman*, Edinburgh
238 Authors
239 By courtesy of Edition Erel, Limoges
240 Authors
241 By courtesy of the Deutsches Museum, Munich
242 By courtesy of Colonel Donald Gill
243 By courtesy of Mr Christopher Monk
244 By courtesy of Mr John Challis
245 By courtesy of Dr Roger Mirrey
246 By courtesy of Mr Noel Mander
247 By courtesy of the Electronic Music Center of Columbia and Princeton Universities
248 By courtesy of Miss Winifred Stevens and the Education Committee of the County Borough of East Ham (photograph by courtesy of Fotofare, London)

MANUSCRIPT SOURCES

32 British Museum, MS Cotton Vesp. A. 1, f 30v
33 British Museum, MS Add. 37768, f 5
35 Cambridge, Trinity College, MS R.17.1, f 216v
37 Ivrea, Cathedral Library, MS 30, f 228v
38 Ivrea, Cathedral Library, MS 30, f 23v
39 Paris, Bibliothèque Nationale, MS Lat. 1118, ff 104, 105v, 106v, 112v, 107v, 110, 111
41 Cambridge, St John's College, MS B 18, f 1
44 Glasgow, University Library, MS U. 3.2, f 1v
47 British Museum, MS Royal 2 A xxii, f 14v

51 Cambridge, Corpus Christi College, MS 16, f 151v
54 British Museum, MS Stowe 17, f 31
56 British Museum, MS Add. 42130, f 164v
59 British Museum, MS Royal 2 B vii, f 229
60 Oxford, Bodleian Library, MS e Mus 65, f 3
62 Oxford, Bodleian Library, MS Ashmole 1523, f 99
63 Brussels, Royal Library, MS 9961, f 66
66 Oxford, Bodleian Library, MS Bodl. 264, f 180v
71 British Museum, MS Nero E II, part II, f 229v

Index of instruments

Index of names

FIGURES IN ITALIC REFER TO PLATES AND CAPTIONS